Soapy
Business

SOAPY BUSINESS:
Through the Mangle!

John Solomon

with illustrations by Ed McLachlan

A Zymurgy Publishing book

First published in Great Britain by Zymurgy Publishing in 2005.

A CIP catalogue record for this book is available from the British Library.

Printed and bound by Bookmarque, U.K.

ISBN 1 903506 14 X

Zymurgy Publishing
Newcastle upon Tyne

To Judy

Acknowledgements

Jo Peel – for her invaluable influence and input.

Michael Moseley – entrepreneur extraordinary and real friendship.

Procter & Gamble Ltd – who took a risk and hired me!

Dr Neil Kelly – who cajoled me into putting pen to paper.

ABOUT THE AUTHOR

John Solomon was born in 1934 in Blaydon-on-Tyne. He worked for Procter & Gamble from 1957 until 1977, when he became a business consultant before taking early retirement in 1985. He became the happiest man alive when he married Judy on 16 December 1961. They have three sons and live in Pinner, Middlesex. His main obsessions are Newcastle Utd AFC and chess, both of which contrive to have similar characteristics – brilliant attack play and lousy defence!

ABOUT THE ILLUSTRATOR

Ed McLachlan was born in Leicestershire. A brilliant and well-respected cartoonist and illustrator, his work has appeared in *Punch*, *Private Eye*, *Housing Today*, *The Spectator*, *Saga Magazine*, *Building* and *The Oldie* to name but a few. He has also worked for most advertising agencies and publishers at one time or another. Ed McLachlan has been named Cartoonist of the Year five times. When not working, he likes to do weightlifting, cycling and gardening as well as investigating his various local pubs. He lives in Leicestershire and is married with three daughters and a son.

CONTENTS

'And yet – proceeding now, to introduce myself positively …

I am a Town Traveller and a Country Traveller, and Am always on the road. I travel for the great House of Human Interest Brothers and have a rather large connection in the fancy goods way.

Literally speaking I am always wandering here and there … now about the city streets, now the country by-roads – seeing many little things and some great things, which because they interest me, I think may interest others.

These are my brief credentials as the Uncommercial Traveller.'

Charles Dickens
1812–1890

The Interview

CHAPTER ONE

Welcome to the Soapy Business

I took a deep breath, checked the contents of my sample bag, stepped out of the car and selected the required point-of-purchase display material from the car boot. Then, taking another deep breath, I set off down the High Street towards my first planned 'solo call': the local retail grocer's store of Mr Cheeseborough and Son; the title emblazoned in large gold lettering on the fascia above the shop window. As I opened the shop door a bell rang, heralding my entry. The owner of the emporium looked up from the bacon-slicer, scowled and continued serving his customer with a benign smile, thereby dismissing my presence entirely! I pinched the side of my thigh to try and eliminate the shaking in my legs, as a nervous spasm seemed to engulf my entire body. While I waited in the corner of the store, I mentally rehearsed the standard sales procedure I had learnt and which I'd practised with my sales trainer over the last two momentous and intensive weeks of training. This had been designed to give me the necessary selling skills and product knowledge, which I could then use to launch myself successfully into the hermetically sealed sales atmosphere of the giant international conglomerate – soap manufacturers Procter & Gamble.

I was in my early twenties, fresh out of National Service and pathologically ambitious to succeed in any employment, provided it enabled me to impress the opposite sex via a motorcar, involved a career which would not entail working at weekends and generated enough funds for me to be able to buy my round of drinks on a Saturday night in the Rugby Club. I was physically fit and healthy, reasonably attractive to women and with sufficient commonsense to realise that whilst a university degree was desirable, not possessing one was not a major handicap when applying for a post in a sales environment.

On 20 October 1957, I applied for a sales representative vacancy advertised in the local Tyneside journal – the *Evening Chronicle*, Box No. 251. It seemed to me that a sales position might well be one that I was suited for. One week later I received an invitation in the post to attend an initial interview with a company called Thomas Hedley & Co. (a Procter & Gamble subsidiary).

My interview the following week was pure theatre, as I attempted to portray myself as an erudite young man possessing the pedigree and potential that major organisations were desperately searching for. The reality was that I had left school with no qualifications, my first employment had been as an office boy on the quayside running errands for the clerical staff of the National Coal Board in Newcastle and my main pastime was supporting Newcastle United Football Club (complete with large wooden rattle, black and white scarf and a strong belief that one Saturday afternoon the loudspeakers in St James's Park would announce that the team was one man short and would John Solomon please hurry to the players' entrance, where the necessary kit would be provided). None of this information I entered in the Thomas Hedley application form staring at me on the eventful day of my interview: Thursday 30 October.

That morning I had awakened bright and early from a sound night's sleep and, galvanised by one of my mother's splendid breakfasts, dressed in my one and only suit of clothes (purchased at a recent sale from Isaac Walton, *the* Newcastle tailor), and with my mother's encouraging interview technique advice ringing in my ears, 'Don't be nervous – just imagine the interviewer sitting before you in his underwear only', set forth from my parents' tiny three-roomed terraced house in Mary Street, Blaydon, a small town located on the banks of the river Tyne, about four miles west of my beloved city Newcastle upon Tyne.

Arriving for my interview appointment punctually, I was ushered into a large well-furnished office, the main feature of which was row upon row of shelving. This displayed the full range of my potential employer's product stable: there were cartons of Oxydol Soap Powder (with a distinctive bright orange background and contrasting black circular patterns), packets of Dreft Detergent (plain green), and boxes of Sylvan Soap Flakes (a rather dull blue). Standing to attention were also several drum-shaped cartons of a scouring powder brand called Mirro, which were next to a display incorporating dozens of bars of Fairy

Household Soap in their distinctive green wrappers. The newly introduced Tide Detergent was displayed on the top shelf – my mother had recently praised the performance of this brand during her traditional Monday washday. Perhaps I could mention this observation to my advantage during the forthcoming interview.

Sprawled in a chair across the office was a miserable-looking, rotund Company area manager, who had discarded his jacket and sported a bilious yellow shirt with orange braces and a purple handkerchief dangling foppishly from the shirt pocket. He greeted me with a limp handshake, reeking of last night's whisky. My dear mother always advised me that at an interview I must proffer a firm handshake, smile and look my adversary straight in the eye – first impressions were of paramount importance. As a result, my apparently 'hung-over' interviewer winced in pain on the handshake, grimaced and slumped back into his chair, avoiding my well-meaning direct eye contact with his heavy-lidded rheumy gaze. His name was John Goodley and I was aware immediately that he was in some discomfort. He appeared to be suffering from what can only be described as a 'subterranean condition', which had him constantly shifting and shuffling his backside whilst seated, and squirming in a haemorrhoid-induced ballet, punctuated with leg-straightening movements and the odd muffled fart!

The interview was to last all of fifteen minutes, and seemed to follow a staccato, somewhat surreal, pattern from the beginning of the introductory shaking of hands (this gingerly) to the unexpected but pleasing 'Welcome aboard!' on its conclusion. During the short discussion, Mr Goodley had glanced casually over my completed application form, which was riddled with exaggerated and inaccurate information equivalent to the pages of a Munchausen diary. I claimed countless school certificates with honours in maths, history, English literature and geography. I professed to be a colossus in local sport – all the 'upper' socially acceptable sports such as rugby and cricket (personifying team spirit), tennis, rowing and polo (highlighting my strengths in individual disciplines). I was also a leading member of the local repertory theatre (in effect I assisted backstage and collected the tickets); I attended church regularly and frequently visited the elderly and infirm in local hospitals.

My 'Billy Liar' obsession was now rampant. My vivid imagination combined with a contrariety of the facts enabled me to present myself with real panache and élan – the ideal candidate, ergo an extremely well-educated, sports-loving, and gregarious applicant of integrity, possessing genuine charitable and Christian qualities. How could I fail? I didn't! Area Manager Goodley arose from his temporary haemorrhoidal throne, shook my hand (gently) and welcomed me to the Company. Of course I accepted immediately, neglecting in my euphoria to enquire about the salary structure. At that moment, my major preoccupation was hoping against hope that no one in the Company would check the validity of my credentials – no one ever did. The eagle had landed!

1 December 1957: so here I was, standing somewhat self-consciously at the rear of Mr Cheeseborough's emporium waiting for him to serve the last remaining customer – and I waited and waited and waited. What I didn't realise at that particular time, but soon discovered, was that there was one traditional unwritten rule in retail selling, particularly in the grocery trade, which was golden – the customer always takes the absolute priority attention of the shopkeeper: however long it takes, the 'rep' must wait until the proprietor deems he is ready to deal with him. Often this meant that when the last customer exited the store, the salesman would have to try to jump in and start his presentation before another customer entered, thus suspending the purchase and selling charade once more. Generally speaking, the grocer seemed to regard the salesman as a necessary evil, treating him with contempt. The grocer relished being able to unleash his pent-up frustrations at the hapless rep – a direct result of having to 'kowtow' to his mainly female customers in order to keep them sweet and persuade them to be regular clients in his emporium.

So, after an interminable amount of time (which at this embryonic stage of my new career I didn't mind too much, as I was able to keep on rehearsing the presentation I had practised in my training sessions), I was ushered forward by the unsmiling Mr Cheeseborough. He queried whom I represented and on learning that I was the rep for Thomas Hedley, soap manufacturers (and before I could launch into my presentation of the merchandise and supporting promotional activity), he growled in his northern dialect 'Nowt today', turned and disappeared into the rear of the store through some plastic curtains. Meanwhile the son (Cheesey Junior), who was filling blue bags with sugar on the side counter, just stood there and grinned, enjoying my humiliation.

I was dumbfounded – all my training sessions had not prepared me for this blunt refusal. I left the store and slowly walked to the sanctuary of my automobile As I sat there in my first-ever transport, surrounded by sales aids, display material and a veritable library of Company documents (including section record books, daily report pads, coupon bags, within which the hundreds of special-offer coupons collected by the retailer were stored, and a Company sales training manual), I panicked. What had I gotten myself into? For all my false credentials and bravado at the interview stage, here I was alone and isolated – the eagle had definitely landed and fallen flat on its beak.

In contrast, and prior to this ignominious introduction to my sales career, my feet had hardly touched the ground during the previous two weeks. I had been allocated a sales area covering North West Durham and extending west, right into the fringes of the Lake District – from a coal mining population to Wordsworth country. I had been issued with a plethora of equipment, Company stationery, sales manuals and, most importantly, a motorcar. Gone were the days of hitching lifts and relying on the Venture Bus Company and my brother-in-law Stan's motorbike. I was a free spirit; the world was my oyster! I could now actually transport Margaret or Maureen or even the snooty Pattie Bagnall directly to their doorsteps instead of queuing at the bus station, inevitably missing the last bus home, and then trudging back many miles to Blaydon, often wet to the skin and looking like some itinerant gypsy.

But, above and beyond all that, a 'minder' had also personally accompanied me for the first two weeks of my employment. This person, officially known as my sales trainer, had been a senior and experienced Company salesman. The sales trainer was responsible for introducing the trainee to the initial sales-training programme (designed to prepare and equip the newcomer to handle all aspects of his designated sales area). In my case this was Alan Claxton, a middle-aged silver-haired Cumbrian who possessed a ready wit and was extremely meticulous in his approach to his training assignments. At this stage it was vitally important for any trainee to impress his minder; it was the trainer's assessment of the progress of his pupil that influenced Thomas Hedley's decision on whether or not to part company with the trainee. It was also essential to establish a good personal relationship with the minder because both parties would be living in each other's pockets for the first two weeks of training. Fortunately, Alan and I hit it off together from day one of the training and we established an excellent rapport – especially as I made sure I laughed in appreciation of his sense of humour (not a difficult task, as his many astute observations often had me in stitches).

My training period mostly involved countless charades and Company documentation familiarisation

THOMAS HEDLEY & CO.
SOAP MANUFACTURERS

SALES TRAINING PROGRAMME FOR—
JOHN SOLOMON · OCTOBER 1957

INITIAL TRAINING PART ONE (CONT)

and therefore it is of paramount importance
for the trainee to retain control of the selling
call at all times, by adhering to the following
format at all times."

STEPS OF THE CALL

1 Planning and preparation.
2 Stock check.
3 Presentation.
4 Close.
5 Display.
6 A/C and records.

SELLING TOOLS

1 Plan slip.
2 Pencil.
3 Sales organiser.
4 Sample.
5 Brand talk.

" The first step of the selling call enables
you to be totally prepared and in a strong position to handle all trade objections to your (CONT)

'Extract from Thomas Hedley Training Manual'

– this was achieved by a form of 'classroom training', initially in the hotel where we were staying and then via actual demonstrations in customer stores by the trainer. The charades consisted of me presenting myself first as the salesman selling to the shopkeeper (a role taken by my trainer), following the script I had memorised the previous evening, and then reversing the roles. In fact, these sessions were extremely intensive and often took place in the car after each demonstration call as well as in the evening back at the hotel. Only after the trainer had decided his pupil was ready would the training end.

The fundamental key to the entire training sessions was to recognise and accept the Company's rigid in-store procedure, irrespective of whatever the shopkeeper did or did not require. In other words, the salesman was expected to plough through his presentation and in-store planned activity, ignoring any objections from the grocery buyer, and then aim to walk out of the store with an order. On reflection, nowhere in the training manual did it advise the sales trainee what to do when the grocer said 'Nowt' and disappeared into the rear of his store.

So here I was facing my first challenge, sitting in my Ford Popular automobile outside the dreaded Cheeseborough Store on Front Street, Barnard Castle. I had read somewhere that selling at all levels often needs an injection of drama into the proceedings to be successful. I therefore resolved to introduce a degree of theatre to my sales technique to achieve some rapport with 'Cheesey'. Accordingly, I decided to ignore my recent 'brainwashing' training programmes, which literally commanded the trainee to rigidly follow specific steps in the store whilst using a predetermined number of sales aids, and thought of a new strategy.

Taking a deep breath, I re-entered the store with resolve and, before my adversary could say 'Edam', I staggered towards the serving counter. Apologising, and with a tremor in my voice, I then requested a glass of water and promptly sat down on the chair in the corner of the store, looking shocked and stunned. The astonished proprietor dropped the cheese-cutting wire from his grasp and, ignoring his 'valuable' customer, dashed into the back shop, reappearing within seconds with a large glass of water. Thanking him profusely, I downed the entire glass and, once again before he could speak, explained with rising excitement in my voice my perceived predicament: I had just moments ago telephoned my lovely wife in hospital and had been told I was the father of triplets! And, as a stranger in town, I just had to share the good news with someone! Instantly the grocer put his arms around me in a congratulatory hug and beckoned me into the warehouse at the rear of the store. There he offered me a glass of sherry (Cyprus), whereupon we toasted the mythical event and the non-existing wife. We were kindred spirits! I duly negotiated a sizeable order for our merchandise and walked triumphantly out of the shop with congratulations ringing in my ears.

On my following month's visit, Mr Cheesey gave me a brown paper parcel – a gift from his emporium – which I found, on opening, contained a box of baby's talcum powder and three pairs of pink baby's bootees (these items I forwarded to my sister Joan who, being married, would no doubt require them long before me). Thereafter I maintained a sound relationship with the Cheesey emporium – though, I have to confess, the continual queries about the triplets did make some of my visits rather short!

The next morning, buoyed with getting through my first day's unsupervised selling calls relatively unscathed, I set forth to meet the challenge of my planned grocery calls for the day with real enthusiasm and anticipation. My monthly workload was designed to cover just over two hundred and forty grocery outlets, which were spread across my sales section, and this committed me to a daily journey plan of twelve selling calls.

My first appointment of the day was in the small picturesque town of Middleton in Teesdale, at the local Cooperative Society, one of the largest retail stores in my sales area. The store traded from a big, imposing sandstone building in the centre of the town, with the Society's name emblazoned in gold letters on the fascia above the shop's large picture windows. On entering through the tall, ornate glass doors with shining brass handles, I was met by a solid wall of jostling female customers, who formed various animated but well-behaved queues at the different serving counters. Unlike with supermarkets today, where self-service is a major part of the modern shopping experience, counter service was the normal way that customers used to be served, be it in a small village grocery or one of the larger Cooperative-style stores. Looking back, it's hard to believe that customers were expected to queue at different counters for various categories of grocery products rather than being able to select all the goods themselves before paying – indeed, even in smaller grocery stores it was rare for a customer to be able to handle the merchandise first (the nearest they got to this was where a store had a company's point-of-sale display unit erected on the shop floor, allowing the customer to actually handle their chosen item before paying – a rare treat!). But in fact this old-style service was a golden opportunity for the locals to catch up on each other's news and gossip whilst they queued. And, although this way of operating was certainly slow and inefficient, such stores frequently became the day-to-day focal point for the local community. Indeed, the biggest problem I had with this style of retailing was that I was always competing with the inevitable queue of gossiping housewives for the proprietor's attention.

I soon discovered that the store in Middleton was constantly busy and that to cope with this it had a highly sophisticated method of processing its customers' payments. Across the shop's ceiling could be seen several metal canisters whizzing and pinging at high speed on a suspended-wire network. These contained customers' cash and invoices and they were constantly journeying to and from the individual serving counters to a small open-topped cashiers' kiosk located in the centre of the saw-dusted shop floor. Here, each individual customer's transaction was checked by a unit of shirt-sleeved, furrow-browed clerical staff, who calculated the cash change and appropriate dividend receipts. These were then swiftly returned to the correct serving counter via a 'flying' canister at record speed and handed to the waiting customer.

It didn't take long for me to spot the grocery manager in his white overall, supervising a small platoon of his brown-coated subordinates, who were busily engaged in filling and weighing various coloured bags with sugar, barley, tea and spices. At the same time, he was also overlooking and checking a small team of perspiring butchers in blue-and-yellow-striped aprons. These underlings were frantically slicing huge sides of ham and bacon on a battery of several red-coloured, manually operated bacon-slicing machines. Having identified the right person, I then spent what seemed to be an interminable amount of time trying to attract his attention, whilst being buffeted by the ebb and flow of the constantly moving tide of chattering, animated housewives who surrounded me.

Eventually, I caught and held the eye of Mr Driscoll, the grocery store manager. What followed was a brief exchange of semaphore signals (it being impossible to conduct a normal vocal introduction due to the intense cacophony from the hustle and bustle of the ever-growing queues of shoppers). The manager beckoned me via the hatch opening of the serving counter to follow him into his small office at the rear of the store. Mr Driscoll was a tall, slim, middle-aged man, who greeted me politely on this our initial meeting. Eager to impress, I found myself somewhat disconcerted by his left eye. As we commenced our negotiations in the oasis of his small office, I couldn't help but notice that the pupil of his eye would begin to recede downwards alarmingly, practically disappear and then slowly emerge back into its correct orbit. I was mesmerised by this optical undulation so much that I carried out the first few minutes of the negotiations gazing in every direction except Mr Driscoll's countenance. However, after a while I came to terms with his disappearing eye and we conducted our discussions face-to-face quite normally.

During our initial conversation, I soon discovered that Cooperative Stores were most reluctant to stock and market groups of merchandise that were in direct competition with their own CWS label brands. No matter how I reasoned with Mr D., he just could not see the benefit; that in selling our nationally advertised brand-leader products such as Daz, Tide and Oxydol alongside his own CWS label brands, his store would be able to offer his customers the choice of the whole soap powder range and consequently would not lose the sales (and profit) from customers buying our brands at his other four major competitors – independent grocery stores located nearby in the town.

For the next twenty minutes we continued to discuss the merits of my presentation, but to no avail. Mr Driscoll failed to understand or accept the logic of my proposition. Finally, as a last resort, I opted for a practical demonstration in an attempt to prove my point. Across from me placed on the corner of the office desk, was a large fruit pie in a foil tray, most probably part of my adversary's lunch. Leaning forward and commandeering the pastry, and with the running commentary, 'This pie represents three thousand pounds' worth of annual turnover of my company's products in Middleton in Teesdale,' I bravely proceeded to divide his pie into four segments. Each, I emphasised, represented the four competitive grocery stores in the town, stressing that this group of stores stocked and sold healthy volumes of our brands. Removing the four pie slices from the tray, I tipped the remaining crumbs onto the desk with a flourish, emphasising that unless his store became competitive in the soap powder market, his share of this lucrative business amounted to no more than a few crumbs.

Mr Driscoll looked straight at me and promptly rejected my 'crumbling' proposition and, with his defective eye moving up and down like a demented elevator, requested one shilling and sixpence for the sliced apple pie! He then pocketed my proffered coins and abruptly bade me good morning. Crestfallen, I trudged back into the store and made my way through the turmoil of shoppers, disappointed that my inspired selling technique had failed. Then, just as I reached the store exit, I was suddenly gripped on my shoulder and an order form was pressed into my hand by the store manager. Mr Driscoll, now smiling, confirmed how much he had really enjoyed our 'buyer/seller' jousting and said he had changed his mind on stocking our brands, perhaps indirectly confirming that the apple-pie charade had worked! The order form had been filled in for small introductory quantities of Daz, Tide and so on. It had taken me over one concentrated hour to win this small order and cost me personally one shilling and sixpence into the bargain, but it was worth it. I thus left the Cooperative store slightly out of pocket but elated with the successful 'pastry-assisted' brand introduction.

Chilly Reception

CHAPTER TWO

In the Bleak Midwinter

I had completed the first six weeks of my new job and was becoming reasonably confident that I could handle the running of my sales section when, out of the blue, I received a missive to present myself at the Company's Sales Office on the following Tuesday at nine o'clock sharp. I had been called to a meeting with our legendary sales manager, Mr Jack William Caygill, who controlled the Company's business across the whole of the North East region via four sales units, each comprising eight salesmen and their area manager. During my short period of time with the Company, I had soon become aware that J.W. was regarded in the organisation with a mixture of awe and fear and was a legend throughout the retail world in the North East. He had a reputation throughout the Company as a tough, hard-working, hard-drinking, down-to-earth sales manager, with a penchant for dismissing employees on the spot – underachievers, poor timekeepers and individuals who fiddled their cash floats, expenses or car business mileage. In short, whilst not a despot, he was not a man to be trifled with. Yet I had been summoned to the great man's presence and I knew not why.

Tuesday morning saw me sitting outside the legend's office door, nervously cradling a cup of coffee made for me by his secretary Mary (who became a great friend over the years and apparently often put a good word in for me when asked her opinion by her boss). Desperately, I tried to conceal my anxiety that someone within the organisation had double-checked my 'glowing' application form and discovered its inaccuracies and false claims – a polo player on Tyneside! – and that over the next few minutes my world would be turned upside down as I was ignominiously dismissed and asked to hand over my Company equipment and, worst of all, my beloved Ford Popular automobile. Such an event would be terrible. I would then have to return to public transport, my brother-in-law's 250cc Calthorpe and long wet trudges back to my home town of Blaydon whenever I missed the last bus home.

My miserable contemplations were rudely interrupted when a deep, resonant Geordie voice shouted from within the confines of the office, 'Get yourself in here bonny lad, we haven't got all day!' My heart lifted. Surely one's executioner would not preface the hanging with the words 'bonny lad' and I entered the sanctum feeling slightly more optimistic and positive.

Sprawled behind a huge desk at the far end of the room was the great man himself. I was somewhat taken aback by his incredible appearance, shrouded as it was by a cumulostratus of tobacco smog. He was wearing a bright-checked suit with a non-matching yellow-ochre waistcoat and his weathered features possessed a healthy glow that was in sharp contrast to his smartly brushed full head of hair, which was shocking white in colour with streaks of custard blond running from each temple to the rear. He also possessed the most riveting blue eyes I had ever seen and these seemed to focus on me with a laser-like intensity. Here, sitting opposite me, was the proven leader, the most successful sales manager in the organisation who, it was rumoured, was not offered a seat on the UK board of Company Directors, despite his skills, because of his strong Tyneside dialect. I later found out that the Procter & Gamble American top management had apparently required an interpreter to assist them at sales conferences!

The telephone on J.W.'s desk suddenly chirped and with a wave of his hand he beckoned me to be seated as he took the call. The interruption afforded me a few precious seconds to consider my situation and strategy. I had sensed on entering Mr Caygill's office that he would see straight through me for the impostor I was and I immediately decided not to try and justify my fraudulent job application form if the subject arose. I would own up to my false credentials and throw myself at his mercy, accepting any degree of largesse he might offer.

Four days prior to my anticipated 'confrontation' with Mr Caygill I had been encountering the most inclement weather – an Arctic storm raged in the North of England and had blanketed the area with several inches of snow. On the Wednesday evening I'd received a telephone call from my immediate boss, John (Twitchy-Pants) Goodley. He had told me he wanted to spend the next day working with me, presumably to monitor my progress following the completion of my initial training period. We agreed to meet in the small market town of Brough at nine o'clock the following morning. Despite the dreadful and often dangerous road conditions, I managed to arrive on time at the agreed rendezvous outside the town post office in the market square. However, there was no sign of Mr Goodley. Though I waited for a good hour, he failed to appear, so, assuming he had been unable to negotiate the difficult road conditions, I carried on with that day's work. One of the calls I had planned was a small isolated grocer-cum-general-dealer's store several miles from the nearest main town. Following many skids and lurches in and out of snow drifts, and with the assistance of a friendly farmer's tractor, I finally arrived at my planned destination. I armed myself with display material, product samples, order book, plan slip, etc., and thus encumbered I staggered into the emporium thoroughly exhausted yet triumphant that I had arrived against the odds.

The owner of the store was a Mr Armathwaite, a rather large and rotund sequacious grocer who followed the customer whom he was serving around his establishment with a benign smile and a rubbing of hands. My mother would have described him as a bit chrisley – a 'Solomon-in-family' term meaning an odious person. After the usual pleasantries about the dreadful weather, I prepared to launch into my presentation, when Mr Armathwaite abruptly announced that he had sufficient stock, required none of my merchandise and bid me good morning! I was flabbergasted. I hastily explained the perilous journey I had undertaken just to get to his store, so that he would give me more of his time.

Recounting the hazardous road conditions – the snow drifts, the farmer's tractor assistance – I then attempted to persuade him to reconsider by resorting to the fund of my often effective, theatrical trade 'objection stoppers' – my pregnant wife with triplets! The once-in-a-year bargain promotional offers – and added, as a final inducement, that the likelihood of the extreme weather conditions prevailing for weeks to come was high. Any order placed today would probably take several weeks to deliver, I pointed out, and he would certainly run out of stock of our merchandise before then. But this was all to no avail: Mr Armathwaite would not budge. So, with a melancholic sigh, I trudged out of the shop and back into the raging blizzard. I checked my watch – from the time I had set forth on this fruitless journey to my exit from the store, two and a half hours had elapsed. In normal conditions it would have taken only twenty minutes. Welcome to the vicissitudes and the cruel world of the grocery trade.

But none of that would matter if I were to be fired. Back in J.W.'s office, Jack Caygill replaced the telephone, cursed, fished out a Woodbine from his gold cigarette case, asked if I smoked and offered me a cigarette (perhaps it was a case of the dying man receiving a last smoke!). He then casually blew a perfect ring of smoke at the ceiling and focused his attention on a document lying on his desk. Declining the cigarette, and with my nerve failing, I decided to take the initiative before the tension became unbearable, and opened the conversation with, 'Apropos my job application form . . .' With a dismissive wave of his smoke-trailing cigarette, J.W. quickly explained that he made it a rule to make contact with all of his new recruits at this stage of their training. To my intense relief he also confirmed his apparent satisfaction with my progress to date. Taking up the document from his desk (which turned out to be the daily report of my sales results of four days ago), he queried the small number of store calls I had achieved that day. I quickly mentioned the atrocious weather conditions that had been prevailing then and mentioned the traumas of the 'Armathwaite' shop journey. J.W. nodded, smiled and expressed how he had experienced similar fruitless remote country selling visits when he was a lowly section salesman many years gone, and that I would soon come to see this as part of a learning curve for the future.

Ten minutes of nostalgia then followed on what life had been like on the road thirty years ago, before he abruptly stood up, shook my hand and said, 'You'll do, bonny lad.' As I made my exit, he surprised me by asking how I was getting on with my area manager, John Goodley. Had I benefited from our training day of four days previously despite the weather? Little realising the significance of my response, I confirmed that unfortunately my area manager had not been able to rendezvous as arranged and that I had completed my work 'solo' on the day in question. I thanked J.W. and exited the office, breathing a huge sigh of relief that I was still an employee of the Company.

On entering the outer office, I saw none other than my immediate boss John Goodley, sprawled in a chair. He was looking extremely uncomfortable, sweating profusely and to my surprise hardly acknowledged my presence. Assuming he was experiencing one of his bad 'subterranean' days, I said a cheery *au revoir* and left the building with a light heart. I was also aglow with the knowledge that my precious Ford Popular and I were to remain together and that the assignation with the snooty Pattie Bagnall for dinner at the Lord Crewe Arms in Bamburgh on Saturday was still on!

I later realised that that Tuesday morning in the Newcastle Sales Office was to be the last time I saw my area manager. Old 'Twitchy Pants' had been fired. Apparently he had falsely asserted that he had worked with me on that fateful snowy day, claimed expenses – lunch and car mileage – and was summarily dismissed from the Company with the traditional Caygill boot up his backside, which on reflection may have aided his medical condition! On leaving the Company he was recruited by J. Lyons & Company, where he rose to become one of their sales directors. So, perhaps my unwitting confirmation of his failure to rendezvous with me on that wintry day and Jack Caygill's right foot did him a favour!

Last Orders, Please!

CHAPTER THREE

Camaraderie

I was born in 1934 in the small town of Blaydon, beneath the gentle slopes of Summerhill (on whose grassy promontory stood a red-bricked rotunda, erected to celebrate the brief nineteenth-century visit to the area, whilst in exile, of the Italian republican nationalist, Giuseppe Garibaldi). Blaydon – or to give its correct name, Blaydon-on-Tyne (situated as it is on the banks of the River Tyne) – was populated by a few hundred inhabitants. Its claims to fame consisted of its link to the Italian guerrilla leader of the Risorgimento, its nationwide reputation for manufacturing fine bricks, and its association with the now defunct 'Blaydon Races' (at one time a famous annual horse-race meeting, eulogised in the celebrated 'Geordie National Anthem').

According to my mother, I had always possessed a confident yet confrontational streak. I once faced up to the exasperated driver of a steam engine on the Newcastle–Carlisle railway line, when I had strayed onto the main track with my pedal cycle; I was just six years old at the time. The bemused fireman who had lifted me into the driver's cab, also offered me a boiled sweet when he deposited me onto the station platform, much to the astonishment of the stationmaster and his staff. I fell in love that day with the mighty steam juggernauts and, despite their virtual disappearance, my affection for them has remained undiminished.

I can trace back my introduction to the world of 'sales and marketing' to the age of eight. It was a late September day and I was in the local store buying some fruit and vegetables for my grandmother, when I noticed that a large display basket of fresh blackberries – priced 1/3d per lb – were of a distinctly inferior quality to the ones I had picked the previous day from the hedgerows nestling beneath Summerhill. So, the next morning I set forth with a large bucket and, after scouring my favourite 'secret' bramble locations, returned home laden down with some superior blackberries. My arms and hands were lacerated with the strenuous effort I had made to reach and pluck the choicest fruit, which annoyingly always seemed to be located in the most inaccessible areas of the hostile foliage. Then, with the help of my dear sister Joan, we selected and weighed the best of the fruit, and packed it into a wicker shopping-basket lined with a thin linen towel (filched from my mother's laundry cupboard).

Self-assured, I set forth to Peter Craig's, the fruit and vegetable emporium located in the centre of town. Mr Craig greeted me warmly as I entered the store, thus boosting my confidence. We were already acquainted, as at that time I was a leading soprano choirboy and Mr C. also sang in the same church choir of St Cuthbert's. After duly presenting my 'merchandise', I explained that if he accepted the total volume – 12lbs of fruit I would guarantee a regular supply until such time as the countryside crops were exhausted. Mr C. bent down and inspected the glistening fruit; nodding in agreement, he smiled and asked me the purchase price. I was stumped; my confidence faltered. I had naturally assumed that on approval, the storeowner would propose his buying price, which I would immediately accept. I mumbled somewhat incoherently that I was not too sure and there and then I learnt my first lesson in retail selling: Be prepared.

Sensing my discomfort, Mr Craig kindly took me to one side and explained the simple, basic rules of retailing – selling price, cost price and profit. I gave it some thought, suggested a price and held my breath. Mr C. agreed and I waltzed out of the store with three shillings tinkling in my pocket. I didn't care that the proprietor had just made a profit of four times that amount; I now possessed the equivalent of six weeks' pocket money! I ran all the way home to break the news to my family – forget being an engine driver, I was going to be a salesman!

Now in this choice career, I was to find that a major component – and the driving force – of a salesman's life was the monthly sales targets. At the end of each month I, together with my seven fellow salesmen, would be summoned to what was euphemistically called the Sales

Strategy Monthly Meeting. The objective was to discuss both the collective and individual sales performances of our sales unit as measured by the Company and to analyse these figures against the preset sales targets. (These figures were taken from data compiled from our individual daily reports, which we had submitted to the Sales Office over the preceding four weeks.)

However, as I soon discovered, the Unit Sales Meeting was really a wonderful excuse for a hedonistic junket, designed to bolster the salesmen's morale and to inject a large dose of camaraderie. By and large the retail salesman was a lonely soul, with only the car heater and a radio programme to comfort him throughout his long journeys, which could often clock up over one hundred miles daily. Therefore, the regular meeting was an important social highlight on the salesman's calendar. Invariably, the monthly sales meeting was an all-day affair; generally to be found located in a grubby room of a hotel or public house.

My first Unit Sales Meeting was held in the town of Barnard Castle at the King's Head Hotel and it set the pattern for all future Company meetings. Though I was a new recruit, the arrival of my participating colleagues heralded an astonishing reunion, especially considering that their previous assembly had been all of four weeks ago. My colleagues piled out of their identical vehicles (black Ford Populars) and immediately engaged in a frenetic theatre of greetings – handshakes, affectionate hugging and much backslapping – giving the bemused hotel guests and bystanders the impression that what they were witnessing must be a unique reunion of ex-members of the Foreign Legion, the only survivors of a perilous desert campaign, who had last met when sharing the dangers of Algeria. The scene in the hotel car park easily surpassed Henri Charriere's Papillonesque description of being reunited with his fellow inmates from Devil's Island.

The good-humoured banter, joking and laughter culminated in a crescendo as we forged our way through the hotel reception area into the lift and then out onto the second-floor corridor, stampeding like young bulls onto the wooden flooring of room twenty-one, our final destination. Although this frenzied camaraderie took my breath away and seemed at the time somewhat excessive, I eventually came to understand that this one day each month was the only opportunity for the lonely soap salesman to share his experiences with a kindred spirit, recharge his batteries and be effectively motivated to confront the dreaded grocer over the next few weeks.

The format for the meeting officially followed the same pattern each month: commencing at 9.00 a.m. sharp, we were led through discussions of our sales performances of the previous four-week period; then we were told the objectives of the coming sales period; and lastly we were given a final summing-up by our area manager. More importantly, the essential 'breaks' in the agenda were religiously adhered to: coffee and biscuits at 10.30 a.m., lunch at 12.30 p.m., tea and sandwiches at 3.30 p.m. I have never experienced since such an orgy of bacchanalia as swept through the break periods. It was as if each salesman was starving, as every crumb of food was demolished and no glass, cup or tankard was left damp. And, if the hotel tablecloths had been flavoured, my voracious companions would have demolished them too.

Indeed, all the food or drink ordered and served throughout the meeting was devoured as if there was no tomorrow. If by remote chance a tomato or a slice of bread or a gingersnap was miraculously overlooked in the general catering melee, the food item was deposited and hidden in the salesman's large leather sample bag, to be consumed presumably when he arrived home! In fact, the main contributory factor for this somewhat unseemly gorging was the knowledge that it was free; all costs were covered by a Company budget. I am convinced that some individuals deliberately went on a diet days before the meeting and rolled out of the hotel with the satisfaction of a sated appetite for the first time in days!

The climax of the entire day, however, traditionally came after the conclusion of the sales meeting with a mass stampede to the hotel bar, the reassuring words 'Drinks are on me lads!' ringing in our ears from our area manager. There would then follow a prolonged raucous bout of serious drinking, with an astonishing range of alcoholic beverages tippled, from spirits to ports and various wines and beers. Everyone quickly became quite merry and were eventually shooed out of the hotel building by the bar staff (who were often made aware of the residential guests' displeasure at the noise and bedlam we created). Exchanging fond farewells, all the salesmen then poured themselves into their Ford Populars and pointed their automobiles in the general direction of home.

I recall one such lively evening during which we were celebrating the winning of a District Sales Competition and on our way into the hotel car park it was noticed that one of our companions was missing. Tramping back into the hotel, a search was made in all the usual places, but to no avail. Eventually we discovered 'Bert', a salesman of some seniority, sitting upright but unconscious on the hotel lift's floor. Apparently he had passed out some ten minutes previously and been transported up and down, up and down, on a series of continuous short elevator journeys, though strangely he had not been reported by fellow hotel residential guests.

I often look back fondly on those wild, liquid days and realise that if today's stringent 'drink and drive' rules applied then, the entire sales force would have had to be disbanded and replaced, as it has been today, with sober, well-mannered, university-educated automatons. Gone for ever are the colourful, swashbuckling pirates of the road, who thought nothing of puking up in the nearest loo, whether it was the gents' or ladies', and then complaining to the hotel staff that the chewing gum purchased from the vending machine in the gents' loo was the worst they had ever tasted – not realising that in their torpid condition they had invested their cash in a contraceptive machine!

Over the months I was to find that I looked forward to the sales meetings as much as my colleagues. In my early days, the meeting was presided over by our recently appointed Area Sales Manager Desmond Cracknell, a former naval aircraft pilot who introduced us to a whole new vocabulary of Service expletives. Unfortunately he was prone to lose his temper with the occasional intransigent grocer and, after a volley of amazing naval barrack-room oaths, he was often reported for his behaviour by the indignant recipient. Indeed, once he was even reported by the North West Durham Federation of Grocers, no less!

Even though Desmond did not suffer fools gladly, whether they were salesmen who worked for him or his seniors to whom he reported, over the time he was our area sales manager we grew to love and admire him, for he galvanised us with his real leadership qualities and drive. It was his relationship to his superiors that was unfortunately to result in his demise, despite his major strengths of leadership and organisation. Desmond's forceful personality was apparently regarded by some fellow senior management colleagues as being overtly ambitious and he was always passed over for higher office, in all probability for being too outspoken and critical of certain aspects of the Company's strategy. Desmond, himself, was also frustrated with the lengthy timescale of the existing promotional ladder operating within the organisation at that time.

Yet it was Desmond who was to have the last laugh over his antagonists. On resigning from the Company after about only five years' employment, he founded his own sales brokerage organisation and became a hugely successful entrepreneur – a multi-millionaire with a private company jet, a string of race horses and a private butler. His lovely wife Freda, whom I met on many occasions whilst they resided in Newcastle, once summed up their relationship: she loved him to bits, but didn't particularly like him. A sentiment often shared by his employees!

Final Try?

CHAPTER FOUR

Next Stop Twickenham!

Shortly before I started my new job with Thomas Hedley & Co. I was introduced to a different type of occupation: the sport of rugby. Over the following months I found that the thrills of the playing field were just as invigorating as the challenges of the selling field. My introduction to this robust sport came, oddly enough, via my mother's hairdresser. The 'Mr Set-and-Perm' of Blaydon, Cliff Prentice, was the proprietor of the only ladies' hairdressing salon in town. The continued existence of this business was entirely due to the salon offering 'tick' or credit to its clientele. Although ostensibly catering solely for ladies, Mr Prentice was also prepared to offer a restricted haircutting service – a mean convict-short back-and-sides style – to his male clients: ones that had been recommended to his salon by their respective female relatives or girlfriends only.

The image Mr Prentice wished to create in the town was undoubtedly that of a high-class lady's fashionable stylist, but his premises and personal appearance were not matched by these ambitions. The salon was a tiny shop opposite the railway station and its cramped interior was adversely affected by its location, being occasionally enveloped in clouds of smoke and soot from the passing steam trains. This was particularly bad during the summer, because Mr Prentice often propped the doors of the salon open. Though the owner always had a cheerful disposition, he did not project a hygienic image: he was small, weedy and spotty, and suffered from halitosis. He always wore the same blotchy, dye-stained white overalls and his myopic gaze was not helped much by his thin, metal-rimmed spectacles with 'bottle top' lenses. Despite all of this, it was only through my mother's recommendation that I was allowed to enter the hallowed confines of Mr Prentice's fine establishment.

My launch into the world of rugby happened on one cold Saturday morning when I was in the salon awaiting my appointment for the 'shilling mow', as it was euphemistically called by the town locals. It was here that I noticed (under a sink basin) an open-topped travelling bag containing various bits of sporting paraphernalia – football boots, red-and-white-striped stockings, towel, etc. On hearing my enquiry as to its ownership, the proprietor strolled over (to the neglect of his female customer) and proudly announced that the sports gear belonged to him: he was a playing member of Blaydon Rugby Club and, despite the traditional Saturday pressure of work in the salon, was off to a match shortly. This was followed by, 'You look a big strong lad – ever thought about playing? Why not come to the match?' I accepted his invitation with alacrity.

The match was Blaydon versus Ryton (a local derby) and involved opposing Junior Fourth XV teams playing with much endeavour but little skill.

Yet I was captivated by the game. It appeared to allow the participants licence to physically assault one's rivals and, provided one could run fast enough, escape the tackles of the majority of overweight lumbering opponents. Sadly for Mr Prentice his services were not called upon that match, being one of the reserves. However, he did perform a neat touch of acceleration sprinting onto the pitch with the oranges at half time.

Unfortunately, despite his enthusiasm for the game, Cliff Prentice only played once for the Fourth XV when a selected player had to cry off at the last minute, and even then he was merely chosen as there was no other alternative. Apparently, during the match towards the end of a closely scored game, the ball landed in his arms and, somehow managing to avoid an opponent's tackle, and bereft of his spectacles, Mr Prentice twisted in the melee of players and set off like a scalded cat towards the try line (much to the astonishment of his colleagues). It was an amazing turn of events as at this late stage a try would mean certain victory. Unfortunately, in his panic to escape his pursuers, Mr Prentice had inadvertently sprinted towards his own try line – accompanied by shouts of encouragement from the opposition and howls of disbelief from his team-mates and the home spectators. Luckily his own fullback tackled him before he could score and the game ended with an honourable draw – but only just!

My own brief introduction to rugby had been all it took to get me hooked onto the sport. I joined Blaydon

Rugby Club without hesitation and, blessed with a useful turn of speed on the field, was soon progressing through the lower XVs. Within a couple of months I had made my debut for the first team, and I played with them for the remainder of my rugby career, until injury forced me out of the game.

Playing rugby at the weekends was also instrumental in relieving the many weekday stresses I experienced on the sales frontline with the man in the brown coat. Whether it was sliding gloriously in the mud, the exhilarating feeling of accelerating through opposing defences to score a try, or the amazing camaraderie after each game (soaking in a steaming, mud-fringed communal bath followed by the traditional raucous, beer-soaked evening), all thoughts of soap powder and the frequent long, weary car journeys were easily banished. These would only emerge slowly the following Monday morning when I was brought back to reality by the tinkling of the grocer's shop doorbell announcing my arrival. Then I would look eagerly beyond the next five days to when I would be able to return to the incredible excitement of playing in the mud again! In some ways, without rugby I would never have been able to keep up with the demanding workload of running my sales sector. Not only did it keep me fit, but over time certain aspects of the game – dodging obstacles (the grocer), spotting openings on the field (seizing opportunities), making touchdowns (negotiating a sale against the odds) – helped me in dealing with my everyday retail opponent: the wily grocer!

It was now three months since my first solo selling call at the formidable Cheeseborough emporium in Barnard Castle. Finally, I began to sense that provided I was prepared to inject live theatre, drama and a sense of humour into my dealings and negotiations with the antagonist in the brown coat behind the counter, and so unhinge myself from the rigid doctrine as directed in the sales training manual, this selling job wasn't too bad after all!

However, there was still a major hurdle facing me as I set out one cold early morning to the market town of Kirkby Stephen, located on the southern fringe of my sales area in North Yorkshire. Whilst the town possessed several small grocery stores, the major retail outlet, which dominated the market square, was a large store with four imposing picture windows displaying a wide variety of merchandise. Parked outside the main entrance were several shop bicycles and a large van bearing the store's logo: 'Braithwaite's – your quality grocer.'

The journey plan I followed every month enabled me to visit each of my customers on a four-weekly basis, and each time I had called at Braithwaite's, the owner Mr Seth Braithwaite had ejected me from his premises with some degree of hostility. Whenever I entered the store and announced that I was the Thomas Hedley soap company representative, the huge-framed proprietor would unceremoniously march me out of his premises and onto the pavement, before disappearing back into his establishment. Yet, on checking Mr Braithwaite's past purchasing record I discovered that up to six months previously he had been the largest volume retail customer across my sales area. What had caused the business to be suddenly terminated?

So here I was again outside the formidable grocer's establishment, which, being a Friday morning, was heaving with customers. I sat thinking in my car, considering whether or not to use the 'Cheeseborough triplets' maternity approach, so successful in my first solo selling call. However, after debating my options, I decided to go for a more dramatic confrontation with Mr S. Braithwaite. After all, what had I to lose? The store had not traded with T. Hedley for many months and the worst that could happen would be another ignominious exit onto the pavement outside Nerving myself, I took a deep intake of breath, grabbed my trusty sample bag, marched through the imposing glass doors and entered the arena.

The interior of the store was a veritable hive of industry: dozens of animated female customers all appeared to be engaged in earnest conversation discussing the price of vegetables or their next-door neighbour's clandestine behaviour with the milkman. Braithwaite's emporium undoubtedly was the largest store in my sales territory. On entering, the customer was confronted by three long serving counters, which formed three sides of a square, and a floor area covered with a carpet of gleaming white sawdust. Behind the left serving counter could be seen a small army of white-smocked shop assistants, furiously attacking huge pyramids of butter and cheese with wire cutters and lethal-looking table knives. Occupied on the opposite serving area were several similarly dressed co-assistants, meticulously filling and sealing hundreds of blue bags with sugar. Standing behind the central serving counter, like a colossus, was the proprietor Seth Braithwaite, busily boning a huge side of bacon with the deft touch and skill of a surgeon.

Mr Braithwaite was a giant of a man, with a ruddy complexion and bovine features, his large head topped by grey curly locks of hair. He possessed a yellow-toothed smile, which he conferred on certain well-endowed female customers whom, according to local town gossip, he would occasionally invite into the rear of the store (on the pretext of inspecting a selected cut of meat in the walk-in freezer) for a clandestine liaison. Apparently it was not unusual to see a smiling and glowing attractive lady leaving the rear of the store with a large carrier bag of best steak and frost sparkling in her hair!

Determined to re-establish Braithwaite's as my biggest customer, I wove my way through the crowded store towards the meat counter and the redoubtable Seth Braithwaite. Greeting him with a cheery good morning as he bent over to examine a side of bacon, I leapt dramatically onto a large display case of tinned food before he could twitch a grimace in my direction.

This manoeuvre took him by complete surprise and gave me a distinct initial physical and psychological advantage: after all, by elevating myself several feet above the proprietor I had momentarily gained the initiative.

There was an instant hush throughout the store as all attention was focused on this odd individual standing aloft, carrying his leather sample bag and confronting a bemused storeowner. My semi-rehearsed words rang out and seemed to echo throughout the emporium and, although my body felt quite numb, I experienced no fear or apprehension. 'Mr Braithwaite,' I said firmly, 'I have been calling on you regularly over the past few months and every time I've set foot in your fine establishment I've obviously been upsetting you, for you've ejected me from the premises. Like you, I have a family to support and a livelihood to make. I'd be more than grateful if you'd advise me as to why I'm so distasteful to you, that you feel you must remove me from your store. Is it my appearance that offends you? Or my overwhelming body odour? Or perhaps I'm always visiting you at an inconvenient time? Whatever it is, please tell me today so I can think about your observations, perhaps correct them and so put myself out of my misery.'

There was a stunned silence: the customers were agog; the blue sugar bags had stopped being filled; the assault on the pyramids of dairy produce had ceased. All attention was focused on the burly figure of Mr Braithwaite. Brandishing the bacon knife in his huge right hand, he looked up at me and, without a word, beckoned me to follow him into the rear stockroom of the store. Inside he pointed me to a large chair next to a desk overflowing with stationery: piles of invoices were clamped on metal skewers and several red ledger books were heaped together. Still without a word he re-entered the front store and left me sitting alone, contemplating what was going to happen next.

Thirty minutes elapsed before the brawny grocer came back into the stock warehouse, where he had left me sitting. Pulling up another chair, he rumbled, 'It's nowt to do with you personally lad, it's the bastard from your company who called on me before you. He overloaded me with merchandise I hadn't agreed to and refused to uplift the surplus stock.' (Later I discovered that my predecessor had deliberately doubled the order in order to win a sales competition.)

Murmuring my apologies, I thanked him for his candour and suggested that if in the future he wished to trade directly with T. Hedley & Co., I would prove to be as honest and trustworthy as my predecessor had been insincere and fraudulent. In response, Mr Braithwaite clamped my shoulder with a huge hand and enquired whether I had any promotional brand offers available. Ten minutes later I waltzed out of the store having reopened my biggest trading account complete with the largest volume order I had ever taken. I was on cloud nine!

It's a Miracle, Madam!

CHAPTER FIVE

Flash – The Wonder Household Cleaner

It was a dismal, wet early February morning as I set forth on my planned sales coverage for the day. The windscreen wipers of my car were working overtime trying to cope with the sheets of rain cascading down from angry sullen clouds. That day I was due in Alston, a quaint small town located high in the Pennine Hills. The weather was such that miniature streams were rushing down the steep cobbled streets, their surfaces resembling black, sculptured layers of perfectly formed, shining, metallic-like dumplings.

The interior of my car resembled a fully loaded, miniature removal van, with cases of merchandise stacked to the roof on the seats both beside me and in the back, making the rear-view mirror superfluous. The car boot was crammed with various items of in-store display material, together with a box of plastic scoops, two squeegee-mops and a large polythene bucket. All of these objects were jammed into the car as a direct result of the sales meeting I had attended on the previous Friday in Newcastle. This meeting had taken place at the prestigious Royal Station Hotel, where only five years previously I had wandered slowly past the hotel's ornate entrance and gazed in awe at the attendant liveried commissionaires whilst on my way to the quayside and my duties as an office boy.

The sales meeting at the Royal Station Hotel was to be my first encounter with the launch and introduction of a product new to the UK market: Flash! According to the accompanying advertising, this amazing product offered to reduce the housewife's kitchen-cleaning drudgery to a minimum, thus enabling her to spend more time shopping in fancy stores like Fenwick's or Bainbridge's or to invite her chums around for a gin and tonic. In fact, the reality was that the majority of Geordie housewives in my sales area shopped at the Cooperative Society and drank stout! Was the North East ready for such a revolutionary product? Judging by the frenetic applause and wild reception from my colleagues throughout the sales meeting, the customers would be queuing overnight to get their hands on it.

Whereas today, Procter & Gamble UK are responsible for literally hundreds of brands across many product categories, way back in 1958 the salesman carried in his sample bag only seven household cleaning products: three detergents (White Tide, Daz and Dreft), one soap powder (Oxydol), a soap-flake brand called Sylvan, Mirro scouring powder and the pioneer product of the UK company – Fairy Household Bar Soap. So the event of an additional brand being added to the product stable was always going to generate great excitement within the organisation, particularly as it also introduced a totally new concept into the market.

Flash was the latest wonder household cleaner and the fervour with which it was introduced was dazzling. The new product launch meeting literally took my breath away and from the moment I entered the meeting room in the Royal Station Hotel to my departure some eight hours later, I was mesmerised. This was my first experience of a district sales meeting and it involved all sales personnel covering the North East region of the UK (which, including around the forty salesmen together with the various line managers and members of the advertising department, meant that the meeting was host to around sixty employees).

When I entered the large meeting room, the hullabaloo and cacophony of sound was overwhelming. As a junior member of less than one year's Company experience, I felt rather intimidated and apprehensive. The District Sales Meeting followed the similar but smaller pattern of our Unit Sales Meetings. However, this larger gathering of salesmen generated a frenzied and vibrating theatre of raucous welcoming shouts, back-slapping and hugged greetings of immense proportions.

After the usual scrummage for coffee and biscuits (in which I managed to secure a single gingersnap before the remaining biscuits disappeared in seconds, many straight into the pockets of several seemingly malnourished individuals), the meeting was called to order via a thump on the table from our leader, the ubiquitous Jack Caygill, our revered District Sales Manager. The entire proceedings were then carried out in the manner of an American spiritual revival meeting. As the Flash advertising team handling the presentation unveiled their brand launch agenda (most of which completely baffled me as they talked in a seemingly alien language, discussing 'above-and below-the line expenditure', 'socio-economic categories' and 'consumer penetration and distribution' as measured by some Norwegian called Neilsen), I appeared to be the only member of the audience who could not understand what on earth this commercial gibberish was all about.

The meeting was presided over by an executive from Head Office, who was attired in a suit of clothes matching the colours of the Flash carton – loud bright greens and yellows! To my mind he looked somewhat ridiculous as he cavorted across the makeshift stage, extolling the virtues of the brand. In addition to the Flash brand group presentation, there were contributions from various Company departments: Research and Development, Manufacturing, Product Distribution and Sales Merchandising. Every superlative used supporting the brand launch was greeted by roars of enthusiastic approval from the captive and animated audience all around me. The mood was electrifying, with only the jingling tambourines of an Alabama spiritual choir missing!

Sitting in this heated atmosphere, I felt out of place next to the mature and perspiring senior salesmen who were standing up and hollering their approval. Punching their clenched fists into the air, they responded enthusiastically to the boasts of the man in the green and yellow suit about how we, as a company, were on a crusade to 'smash' our competitors with our unique product and that, thanks to Flash, the British housewife would forever be in our debt for saving her future years from the slavery and drudgery of the kitchen. Alleluia! The Lord be praised!

In contrast, I noticed that our sales leader, Jack Caygill, sat almost impassively at the top table, chain-smoking his Woodbines. After thirty years with the Company he must have seen it all before and if there was any expression on his face at all, it was a slight amusement at the theatrical din and frenzied atmosphere. Perhaps, like me, he was not a religious man – commercially that is!

Prolonged applause finally brought the launch meeting to a close. We then all divided into our own individual sales units for different planning sessions, where product samples of the new revolutionary brand, together with items of supporting in-store display material, were distributed. After that I took my leave thankfully and, with my head still spinning, headed for my parked car. Driving slowly through the damp streets of the city towards my home and relative peace, I contemplated the following Monday with some apprehension.

So there I was in the market town of Alston, at my first sales call, ready to convert the masses to the way of Flash. The shop I was visiting was called Armstrong's, a medium-sized family grocer's run by two brothers and a small number of shop assistants. I was fortunate to be able to park immediately outside the store, as any further away and my bulky equipment and I would have been saturated by the 'Pennine' storm that was engulfing the town.

As I entered the store, the many customers and staff who glanced in my direction saw a young chap manfully juggling with various items of equipment: a large leather sample bag, one medium-sized plastic bucket, one squeegee mop and several display cards. With such a captive audience I felt I had entered stage left and was ready to perform. Let the entertainment roll!

In order to achieve maximum trade acceptance of our new brand, we had been told at the Flash launch meeting that each ,salesman must give a practical demonstration of the product's performance in every outlet. By doing this we would be simulating and illustrating the domestic conditions encountered regularly in the kitchen by the UK housewife. So, resembling a Wild West snake-medicine travelling showman, I theatrically beckoned the throng of now curious customers and staff to the centre of the large tiled shop floor, at the same time requesting the nearest shop assistant to fill my plastic bucket with water, preferably warm. Using the plastic scoop provided, a carton of Flash and brandishing the squeegee mop, I then proceeded to dramatically demonstrate the efficacy of this new wonder 'once over' household cleaner with startling results.

As all trading in the store had by now ceased, I was amazed at the success of my own effrontery. Everyone was focused on my demonstration with a mixture of amusement and incredulity. I mopped away vigorously and within seconds the small treated area of grimy mosaic tiles was transformed, with all the original coloured patterns shining as new. It had worked! A ripple of applause broke out from the surrounding captive audience, together with a saucy comment from a large buxom woman asking if I would be willing to repeat the cleaning exercise in the sanctum of her kitchen and what would be my fee.

With the demonstration successfully completed, I began to gather up my equipment and collect my thoughts for my negotiations with the storeowners. Following the success of act one, scene one, and the tacit approval from the store's customers, I felt confident that Messrs Armstrong and Co. would be quite positive in their acceptance of this new brand. The elder of the two brothers, Seth Armstrong (a somewhat taciturn and morose individual), stepped forward and rumbled, 'Now that you've shown up shop to be dirty and unhygienic, I'd be obliged if you'd finish job properly and clean rest of floor with your "wonder" product!' Unable to believe what I had heard, I thought at first that he was teasing me. However, Seth Armstrong's hostile demeanour quickly convinced me that he was being deadly serious. So with little alternative, and in order to preserve the personal goodwill of one of my larger retail customers, I set to and commenced to 'Flash Mop' the remainder of the huge shop floor. Some twenty minutes later I had completed the onerous task, with much sniggering and joshing from the shop assistants, and I turned expectantly to the owners. But there was not to be the happy ending to my in-store drama that I had hoped for. Seth Armstrong, arguing on the grounds that few people in the town possessed kitchens that had the space or surfaces to warrant investing in such a 'fly-by-night' product as Flash, said that in his judgement his customers would prefer to continue using their trusty bar of household soap. I was astonished. He rebuffed all my attempts to convince him to accept the product and eventually I retreated from the store disappointed, frustrated and angry, vowing to blow up his shop if I could only get my hands on some dynamite!

However, all my efforts were not to have been in vain. On my following monthly visit to the store, Seth Armstrong admitted he had made a mistake on my previous call. Rejecting my Flash demonstration had meant that he had lost out on the redemption of hundreds of 'money-off' Flash coupons which had been circulating throughout the town. In consequence he had also lost many customers and much profit to the rival stores in town who had accepted stocking the brand on my 'cleaning presentation' (and fortunately, unlike the Armstrongs, had not insisted that I act as a professional 'Mrs Mop'). So I got my order for Flash from the Armstrongs after all. Ah, the trials and tribulations of the travelling soap salesman!

The Training Run

CHAPTER SIX

Feathered Companions

It was a delightful early spring Monday morning when I set out for my scheduled day's work, which would take me to the perimeter of my sales section and the dozen or so small village retail shops located in the rolling countryside west of the market town of Hexham. The rear and passenger seats of my vehicle were packed full of equipment, including product samples, point-of-purchase display cartons for placement on the retail store's serving counter and the usual paraphernalia of stationery. However that day, if one was to glance into the recesses of the car boot, it would be unusually clear of all Company equipment. Instead, accompanied by a cacophony of squawking, cooing and a flapping of wings, lay a large wicker basket containing a couple of dozen racing pigeons!

'Solomon and Son' – my father and grandfather – were well-known fanatical racing-pigeon fanciers in the North East and, prior to the commencement of the racing-pigeon season, exploited every method they could conceive to train their birds to the peak of fitness. As a result, whenever a daily sales journey involved travelling a distance in excess of forty or fifty miles (two or three times per month), the Thomas Hedley company car was commandeered by Solomon and Son. I would be instructed by my father to transport and release the feathered merchandise from a specific rural district at an agreed synchronised time. Whilst I was uncomfortable with this 'family' carrier arrangement – as it was strictly against the Company rules, which forbade the use of the vehicle for non-Company use during working hours – I was powerless to extract myself from this activity. My father had a strong persuasive personality and convinced me of the glory and honour to the family name which would be achieved via my contribution to that season's training programme!

My father, Jake, was the third child of a coal miner in the village of High Spen (located in the hills a few miles south of Blaydon). The family had been settled there for many years and, according to my mother, were regarded in the region as hardworking, reliable, honest and totally dependent on the local colliery for employment and income. The exception to this was my grandfather, who was a shot firer down the pit – a most dangerous job, which required consummate skill in the handling of explosives deep in the dark, wet chasms of the earth. He astonished everyone in the village when, at a time of major regional unemployment, he resigned from his guaranteed 'job for life' and opened a fish 'n' chip restaurant instead. (Rumours were rife at that time regarding the financial source of my grandfather's sudden ability to purchase the business for cash, and these centred on his 'friendship' with a rich widow who resided in a detached house in Wylam – which was reputed to have an inside toilet; the height of luxury).

For the first few years of their marriage, my parents lived above the shop and it was here that I was born. (To this day my favourite meal has always been haddock and chips, and I can place this right back to the location of my birth.) With a growing family, my father (a bricklayer by trade) soon moved his family to a nearby small terraced house located on the steep slopes of Blaydon, where we lived for the next twelve years or so. However, he still shared a consuming passion with his own father: racing pigeons! This hobby transcended all other family, social and sporting activities. The 'burds', as my father would say, required maximum priority. Where he steadfastly refused to lift a broom or a cloth domestically, the pigeon loft or the 'ducket' was religiously cleaned (often twice daily). The pampered birds were fed, watered and exercised every day and I was conscripted to carry out the early morning pigeon-loft duties, often arriving at school with my satchel covered in bird droppings and feathers in my hair.

However, these extremely high standards paid off, as Solomon and Son built a reputation as one of the most successful pigeon fanciers in the Northern Counties. They were the proud winners of many races, but they had never won the prestigious Amalgamation Beauvais National Race Trophy (akin to the Cup Final in soccer). This was the top event in the Northern Counties' racing-pigeon calendar. To win this race a pigeon must fly over four hundred miles from the French town of Beauvais to the North of England. A truly challenging competition, winning the trophy would be a dream come true (not to mention that there was also a substantial cash prize given to the victor).

I recall it as if it was just a few days ago! The great day had arrived: the Beauvais National Trophy. My father – as befitting a cup final! – dressed smartly in his only suit and freshly laundered open-collared white shirt (no tie) and, sporting the new tweed cap purchased just for today's race, departed on his bicycle to the allotments, a scenario being repeated throughout the North East. A handler had already carefully taken the pigeons to Beauvais and, once released, the start time had been officially recorded and telegrammed to England. A copy of this telegram was then displayed locally and from this the pigeon-fancier could calculate the estimated time of arrival of his own pigeons in his area.

That day I cycled down to the allotment in time to capture the pre-atmosphere of the Beauvais – or 'Bovaz' as pronounced in the local Geordie dialect. It was generally agreed that the first racing birds would appear no sooner than around 6 p.m. So at just after 4.30 p.m. Solomon and Son went off home for their teas before returning in good time for the arrival of the first competitors.

Alone – and in charge – I entered the pigeon loft and glanced at the pigeon clock, which would record the bird's finish time. This worked by having the newly arrived pigeon's racing ring deposited inside it, triggering the official – and tamperproof – time of arrival. It was 5.20 p.m. and in ten minutes or so I could anticipate hearing the rattle of my father's bicycle speeding down the outside path. My excitement was increasing, as the moment our pigeon arrived home was a momentous event. Not even the prospect of seeing the Three Stooges film at the Plaza Cinema after church choir practice could distract me from the entrancing possibility of us winning the Beauvais Trophy.

Suddenly I heard a raucous cacophony emanating from the allotments of our neighbouring competitive lofts. The distinctive signal of the rattling of bird-feeder tins, followed by individual owners' various-pitched whistling, was a significant indication that perhaps a 'Big Race' contestant had been spotted. I rushed out of the loft and squinted into the sky. At last I saw a tiny far-off dot heading in our direction, yet it wasn't even half past five. What if the distant, fast-approaching bird was heading for our loft? I was alone and I had never been allowed to time-clock a racing bird.

The little dot in the sky got larger and larger and, as it descended like a predatory kestrel, the now discernible outlines of a racing pigeon plummeted towards our garden. With a flurry and clapping of wings, it landed in a heap on the wooden landing platform of the loft. Instinctively I rushed forward and swept up the feathered racer in my hands, who too exhausted, offered no resistance. Having witnessed the 'clocking-in' procedure numerous times, I removed the vital race identity ring nervously and successfully recorded the arrival time.

Ten minutes later the garden gate swung open and my father arrived, unaware of the preceding activity, and casually mentioned in his normal monosyllabic way that I should go home for some tea. Spluttering in my elation, I told him what had happened. Initially he ignored the rising excitement in my voice and then accused me of pulling his leg. Going into the loft, a few seconds passed before I heard, 'You bugs of Hexham! Wore John's cum up trumps!' and with that he jumped down from the platform and gave me a huge hug, whilst at the same time checking to see if I had carried out the required 'clocking-in' procedure.

This was the first (and only) time my father demonstrated any outward sign of affection towards me and I found myself highly embarrassed. However, the 2/6d reward he gave me (five weeks' pocket money) quickly took my mind away from his embracing hug. I cycled home at great speed to announce the afternoon's events to my mother and sister, but refrained from mentioning the cuddle to them, believing it would tarnish my father's image of a tough, no-nonsense Geordie.

The following week, after all the racing times throughout the North East Amalgamation had been checked, the results were released and it was duly announced that the 1948 winner of the Beauvais Trophy was . . . Solomon and Sons of Blaydon!

So, back as a grown man with an automobile, I was now being seconded to help with the training of these champion pigeon contenders using my car. As I neared the town of Alston, high up in the Pennine Hills (some fifty miles from my home town and the agreed release point), I looked around for an open meadow devoid of electricity pylons – a hazard to racing pigeons – and parked the car. Opening the boot, I lifted the birds' basket out onto the grassy field and checked my watch before starting to open the basket lid. Just then, with a growl of thunder in the distance and the fast-darkening sky heralding a storm, there was the pitter-patter of heavy raindrops bouncing off the car roof. I quickly put the pigeons back in the boot, it being folly to liberate the flyers into an electrical storm where they could become easily disorientated and lost for ever. The birds were annoyed and frustrated: sensing that the release for their homeward journey was imminent, they squawked their disapproval at the closing boot lid. Unable to release the pigeons, I had no option but to carry on with my sales calls, hoping that the storm would blow itself out and give me another opportunity to let them go later.

However, the torrential rain did not abate. Conscious that I had to get the birds back to the sanctuary of their loft as quickly as possible, I decided to accelerate through my workload for the remainder of the day, hopeful that I would not lose the effectiveness of my selling calls. I also phoned my father to explain and was given detailed instructions on the maintenance of the birds' comfort and welfare.

Having visited eight of the twelve stores planned for that day, it was now lunchtime and I stopped in the village of Allendale to get some provisions. My car received many quizzical looks from passers-by as they walked past its melodious boot! In the local village store, Mrs Robson (the shop proprietor) finished serving a customer before coming over to me. After selling me two homemade meat pies and a sausage roll for my lunch, she asked, 'Anything else, bonny lad?' With a bold face, I requested a small plastic bowl, two packets of haricot beans, a bag of dried maize and a small packet of peas. Bemused, she collected and packaged my 'lunch' menu, which I paid for. Then, looking even more stunned, she disappeared into the rear of the shop with the plastic bowl on my request for some water. Reappearing with her equally confused husband carrying the bowl of water, they presented me with my 'snack lunch'. Thanking them I left the store, but not before overhearing their whispered remark, 'Don't young people have funny eating habits these days!'

I eventually arrived back home that day a couple of hours earlier than normal, with the pedigree racing birds apparently none the worse for their incarceration. Once they had settled down, they seemed perfectly happy in the basket. However, I was relieved to be able to return them to their loft after their flightless journey to Alston and back (via my various store calls). That following weekend Solomon and Son won the prestigious Northern Counties Trophy in record time – this despite the winner's interrupted training programme and unusual snack lunch! And it warms me to think that perhaps the several Thomas Hedley 'unscheduled' country field training visits, involving my feathered co-passengers, contributed to the success of some of the best racing pigeons in the North of England at that time!

Sweet Encounter!

CHAPTER SEVEN

Demerara Sugar

It was late September. I had survived nearly a year of the rigours and pressures of working for an organisation with a reputation in the grocery manufacturing trade for a rapid turnover of sales personnel. Unlike some, the longer I was in the job, the more I found I enjoyed the cut and thrust of the field sales operation, despite the many confrontations I experienced with the man in the brown overall behind the counter. It was a late Friday afternoon as I neared the delightful Cumbrian town where I had my next appointment. I was driving down along the narrow country lanes from Penrith, enjoying the beautiful farming countryside and, with the car windows wide open, breathing in the balmy, intoxicating atmosphere of rural Cumberland. We were experiencing a glorious and long Indian summer, with the temperature hovering around the mid-seventies and, contrary to Company dress code, I had discarded both my jacket and tie. Feeling relaxed and contented, I drove down the steep roads and entered the town.

My one and only customer in the area was the local Cooperative Society, which operated a medium-sized grocery store as well as several Coop delivery vans which serviced the many outlying farms and the agricultural community in general. The general manager of the

Society was a Mr Tallentire. He was assisted in the grocery department by the lovely Mrs Tallentire, who was responsible for ordering all the merchandise.

On seeing the delectable Mrs Tallentire during my first visit to the store, I fell in love. Her first name was 'Tessa', she was in her mid-thirties and she exuded sex in everything she did, combined with a rare innocence and naivety that only made her more desirable. I remember my biro used to shake visibly as I wrote down the details of our agreed order, but she never seemed to notice my discomfort. With a toss of her long Titian hair and a smile toothpaste manufacturers would have loved to incorporate into their TV commercials, she would shake my trembling hand on conclusion of our negotiated business and wish me a pleasant journey home.

That Friday, hot and sticky from the car, I entered the store, which at 5 p.m. was devoid of customers. Surprisingly there were also no staff visible behind the serving areas. After a few moments I shouted 'Shop!' to gain some attention and soon after I heard light footsteps running across the floor above the ceiling where the store warehouse was located. After a few seconds the gorgeous shape of Mrs Tallentire appeared, slightly out of breath. She greeted me with her customary friendly warmth and quickly explained that she was the only member of staff on duty, her husband being out with the delivery teams and her normal assistants having left early for the day. Tessa had discarded her normal white store overall and looked absolutely stunning in a low-necked green blouse with matching skirt, her hair piled up on top, creating an image which would have taken Hollywood by storm. Seemingly unaware of my regard, she walked past me and locked the shop's front door, which was rather unusual. Then she beckoned me to follow her up to the warehouse – an even more surprising event as we normally negotiated the order in the confines of the store. As we climbed the creaky wooden staircase I was intoxicated by a cloud of that oh-so-familiar Lily of the Valley, and beneath that something more acrid: an odour reminiscent of one I had smelled at the entrance to a fox's lair in Stella Woods, near my home in Blaydon.

As we climbed the narrow staircase, our thighs brushed gently against each other and a frisson began to stir throughout my entire being. The warehouse was as wide as it was long, with rows and rows of cardboard boxes and large wooden crates containing a variety of merchandise. Against the far wall I noticed several large jute sacks containing demerara sugar, which were stencilled with the name of some distant plantation in Guyana. It was towards this area that the delectable Tessa motioned and guided me without a spoken word. Other than a squeaky floorboard and the bellowing of a cow in some distant field, the warehouse was cloaked in a cathedral-like silence, punctuated only occasionally by the idle chatter of some swallows in the eaves discussing their imminent journey and best route to southern climes.

Without any warning, but with an enigmatic and demure smile resembling the famous *La Gioconda*, Mrs

T. slowly and deliberately undressed before me. Then, reclining naked on the warm hessian bed of undulating brown sugar, she beckoned me forward. I was in a complete trance as I shuffled towards this beautiful vision, somewhat ungainly trying to disrobe casually en route to the most magical and mystical moment of my life. We made love tenderly yet passionately: I was in a surreal state of utter bliss. The only witness to our union were thousands of tiny dust particles, which danced and floated slowly down in the bright shaft of light from the skylight immediately above us, like magical confetti cascading down and celebrating our union. At last, at the age of twenty-two, I was no longer a virgin. I was in heaven – life couldn't get any better!

However, as we lay together entwined in a soporific intimacy, our tranquillity was interrupted by the sound of a vehicle entering the rear courtyard of the store, followed a few seconds later by the unmistakable sound of a key being inserted into the large rear door of the building. We leapt from our hessian nest as we heard the call of 'Tessa!' ringing through the building. It was Mr Tallentire returning unexpectedly earlier than anticipated. I later calculated that it took no less than twenty seconds to collect our strewn items of clothing, get dressed and walk totally composed down into the store! Mr Tallentire came into the shop as I pretended to agree an order for delivery as soon as possible, wildly brandishing an order pad and flourishing a biro. It was only after I waved goodbye to the Tallentires and reached the safe haven of my car that I realised I was devoid of my Y-fronts!

The following month, my next, eagerly anticipated appointment to see Mrs Tallentire proved to be a huge anticlimax. Although I was greeted warmly by the wondrous Mrs T., there was no hint of our previous momentous encounter; it was as if it had never taken place. My only consolation came as I was about to leave, when Tessa handed me a small brown paper parcel tied with coloured ribbon. Puzzled, I unwrapped the package once I was in my car and found a pair of neatly laundered Y-fronts! Also in the parcel was a small bag of demerara sugar together with a card scented with Lily of the Valley, which simply said 'Tessa'. For many months afterwards I slept with the small bag of demerara under my pillow, dreaming of the magical event when I finally gained my manhood. And, as a direct result of that life-changing momentous occasion, I find that whenever I see some demerara sugar, be it on a restaurant table or in the kitchen cabinet, I am transported back to that sultry, magical, late autumnal afternoon in Cumberland – and the delectable Mrs Tallentire.

OK! I'll Come Quietly

CHAPTER EIGHT

A Fair Cop

When I joined Thomas Hedley & Co. in November 1957 and was given responsibility for Sales Section no. 103, my first two weeks had been spent in the comfort of the King's Head Hotel, Barnard Castle, at the Company's expense. Thereafter I was expected to find my own accommodation, ideally centrally located and adjacent to the majority of the retail customers within my designated sales section. After some thought, I chose to live in the town of Bishop Auckland. This would enable me to return to my home base on the completion of each day's work, with the only exception being a required two-day overnight stay in the George Hotel, Penrith, when covering the far corner of my section in the Lake District.

So, once I had finished my initial two-week sales training period, I arrived in Bishop Auckland to search for immediate lodgings. As I drove up the steep hill into the town, I noticed a rather attractive female police constable sauntering along just ahead of me. Braking quickly, I pulled up beside her, wound down the car window and attracted her attention. Working on the principle that perhaps the town constable would have a reasonable in-depth knowledge of the area, I enquired if she could kindly recommend any suitable digs within the town, adding that I was pretty desperate, requiring them immediately. PWC Allan (Joan, I later found out, as I was to date her within a couple of weeks) leaned forward through the car window and, with a devastating smile and the most attractive penetrating blue eyes (which I immediately fell in love with), directed me to a house called 'Skelmorlie': a large Victorian detached building in the residential part of town, which I couldn't miss as the entire house was rendered in a bright green stucco.

Skelmorlie was to be my home for just over a year. The guesthouse proved to be a clean and comfortable abode and was run with military precision by two middle-aged spinsters – Miss Bell (a tall, thin, angular woman who needed to shave) and Miss Farthingale (a small female dumpling with unfortunate BO, who dressed in Bohemian attire and quoted Shakespeare whenever she wanted to emphasise a conversational point). My fellow guests were young, raucous police cadets on secondment to the local police station for training purposes, who proved to be wonderful companions. Messrs McAlister, Brown and Jones were mischievous rogues, all with a delightful sense of humour and forever performing practical jokes often to the irritation of our sedate hostesses. Apart from the cellophane toilet-seat jape and the apple-pie beds prank (good for playing on an unsuspecting person who's had one too many to drink, this involves folding the person's bottom bed sheet in half, thereby shortening the inside of the bed, much to the consternation of the victim), the ongoing deception was to throw a teaspoon into the overgrown rear garden, surreptitiously, two or three times a week after the evening meal. This mystified the owners, who were frequently at a loss to explain the disappearance of their teaspoons and were often seen in the local hardware store purchasing replacement utensils. Fortunately, during our period of residence the garden was never cultivated, being left to grow wild. We often tried to assess the sheer volume of teaspoons that must have been concealed in the undergrowth, speculating on the reaction of Mistresses Bell and Farthingale were the grass and brambles ever to be cut back by some unsuspecting gardener.

By the time my twenty-third birthday rolled around, Bishop Auckland was my adopted home town. On that bright late summer's morning, I set forth on my day's selling calls with a jaunty step. I had received several birthday cards in the early morning post, which had pleased me greatly. As I read the greeting cards at the breakfast table, my fellow guests made no comment or acknowledged my birthday and this had puzzled me somewhat. Still, it was a glorious day, and as I made my way to my first stop on the High Street, my mind was focused on the day ahead. The thoroughfare was crowded with Friday shoppers, looking for weekend bargains, and the last thing I expected was to be manhandled from behind and wrestled to the pavement. Without any warning, I felt the snap of handcuffs on my wrists, followed by the exclamation, 'Got you at last!' I turned over to see three hefty uniformed constables – my fellow chums from Skelmorlie who had vigorously apprehended me! They then proceeded to frogmarch me down the centre of the High Street to the astonishment of the passers-by, who presumably regarded me as an escaped criminal justifiably being arrested and en route to the town clink!

On reaching the local police station and despite my vigorous protests – 'Come on fellas, a joke's a joke and I've work to catch up with!' – I was marched in front of the duty desk sergeant who, dead-pan, proceeded to go through the booking-in procedure, charging me with resisting arrest and the use of foul language. He then took my fingerprints and escorted me to a subterranean cell, where for the next hour I languished in solitary confinement.

Suddenly the heavy cell door swung open and standing there were three laughing uniformed musketeers, together with the desk sergeant. They were holding a large, candle-lit cake and proceeded to sing a chorus of 'Happy Birthday'. After a slice of cake, I had to agree it had been a realistic and cunning 'sting' and I was subsequently released with all criminal charges dropped. Still, I promised myself revenge sooner or later.

Such an opportunity came after a few weeks when I was once again strolling down Bishop Auckland High

Street, having completed my selling calls for the day. Ahead of me I noticed my uniformed antagonists and I realised this was the perfect chance to get my own back. Creeping up behind them, I knocked their helmets off unceremoniously into the busy road, to the astonishment of the passers-by! Whilst they attempted to retrieve their headgear rolling and bouncing amongst the passing traffic, I was able to sprint to my car and accelerate away, fiendishly laughing in delight at being able to return the favour.

Over the evening meal that night, we agreed on a truce and to tone down the practical joke activities. However, this did not apply to the hidden mountain of teaspoons, which continued to expand in the wilderness at the rear of Skelmorlie!

Exposure!

CHAPTER NINE

Oops!

Several months had elapsed since my birthday 'incarceration' and I had really begun to get into my stride running my section of the sales operation. I was thoroughly enjoying my career, and this was reflected in the growing number of sales I was generating. As a direct result of increasing the overall Company business of Thomas Hedley brands sold across my sales section (or 'volume' as it was colloquially called within the organisation), I found myself winning several sales-incentive Company competitions. I netted some useful prizes such as golf clubs and various car accessories, and some less than useful such as kitchen or gardening equipment (the latter I would flog to colleagues who were married and possessed a garden).

My sales unit consisted of two young bachelors (myself and my great mate and rival John Scott) and five other salesmen who were married with families to support and mortgages to negotiate. Without the burdens of domestic responsibilities, I was a free spirit and I was determined to enjoy my liberty before settling down and joining the ranks of the lawn mowers and nappy changers. Being in my early twenties and a fit, six-foot-tall rugby player with an appealing countenance and a sharp sense of humour

– not to mention my possession of the essential motor vehicle – all served to strengthen my charms with the opposite sex. My social status in the 'market place' was also further enhanced by my occupation: I was a young man going places, employed by the prestigious Procter & Gamble Ltd. – an international company tagged with the reputation throughout the region as a major blue chip organisation.

Confident in my pursuit of female company, I soon hit the veritable jackpot and met a fabulous girl, Margaret Oliver – a young schoolteacher with a showbiz attitude to life. Margaret was an effervescent blonde with a great figure, a leading lady in an operatic company and she had a personality and frisson that, combined with her sexy smile, guaranteed her maximum attention from her many admirers. Even at the local dances, men would queue up just to be near her. In fact, she could best be described as the 'Bette Midler' of the North East. And I got lucky!

Margaret and I met at a party just as she was ditching her current 'clingy' boyfriend, and we hit it off immediately. Over the following year I was transported into a wonderful, torrid relationship. One of my most vivid recollections of our stampede through the social calendar of the North East was our attendance at one of my rugby club's Saturday night buffet-and-dance events. That evening we arrived quite late for the function and the band was just finishing off its pre-interval spot. Fellow rugby player chum Jim Huxley, who was organising the musical entertainment, produced a gramophone record

82

featuring the great Chris Barber and his jazz band (whose music was often played during the interval break of the non-melodious resident three-piece band). Margaret – whose entrance into the clubhouse was greeted first by a hushed silence and then a chorus of whispered ribald comments – was in a fabulous, low-slung, eye-catching green silk sheath dress. She seemed to suddenly come alive when she heard the opening strains of 'Whistling Rufus' and, grabbing my hand and promenading us to the centre of the dance floor, began to gyrate rhythmically to the high-tempo beat of the fast jazz number. No one joined us on the dance floor: the staff behind the bar stopped serving, all the smokers left their cigarettes and pipes unattended in their ashtrays, the ladies in the kitchen preparing the buffet crowded into the serving hatch behind the bar and all drinking ceased. Even Jack Morris, the club's octogenarian president, hustled his way through the crowd's perimeter and perched on a stool to watch. The whole room was focused on the solitary duo in the centre of the floor (although I was really just an appendage) and when eventually Chris Barber came to a halt, the entire place erupted with applause, accompanied by much whistling, pleas and shouts for more. This was all to no avail however. Margaret had completed her performance and, exiting stage left, homed in on the bar, where she was served free drinks for the remainder of the evening.

Unfortunately, there was not to be a happy ending to this tale. The following week, the delicious Margaret ditched me for another companion (not unlike my predecessor, I was too clingy). As a result, whilst my rugby club colleagues continued to regard me as a useful member in rugby-playing terms, I was never really forgiven for depriving the club of the entertaining and exciting 'Bette Midler'.

However, despite my turbulent social life, I was still gaining ground in my career. In my short experience of the 'Soapy Business' so far, I had quickly discovered that it was of the utmost importance to negotiate a correct, balanced order with the grocer. Being able to work out the exact quantity of the Company's stock held in a shop at any one time was therefore vital. Without this stock awareness the salesman was always at a disadvantage during the negotiation, not knowing what would make an accurate order; lacking this information he would be subject to the grocer's purchasing whims on the day. Invariably, the grocer preferred to order as little as possible (wanting to maintain minimum stock quantities only) and so would decline a suggested order on the false grounds of already having sufficient stock, ruthlessly cutting back the recommended order volume. Consequently, he tended to run out of such fast-moving merchandise as soap powder – to the detriment of sales levels. Such out-of-stock situations were a major problem facing most manufactures in the retail grocery trade at the time and the need to overcome such difficulties had been emphasised in my sales training.

So, with a combination of guile, ingenuity and hard-earned mutual trust, I had set about gaining access to the majority of grocery stockrooms across my sales section. I found I could overcome the most obstinate grocers by requesting to check the condition of the store's last delivery of Thomas Hedley products for signs of damage (there never were any). This resourcefulness on my part was reflected in the growing number of sales I was making. However, there was one major retail outlet whose owner steadfastly refused access to his stockroom: Mr Hardcastle, who ran a small but thriving establishment located in the market square of Brough. I began to notice on my monthly visits to this shop that the soap fixtures behind the main serving counter were often out of stock of our major brands. If I could only establish the levels of our merchandise being held in Mr Hardcastle's stockroom prior to our order negotiation it would be a real bonus.

With this in mind, I decided that it was time to take the initiative and make a positive move towards gaining entry to the 'out of bounds' stockroom, which I assumed was located behind the plastic curtains at the rear of the shop. So, on my October visit, I strode forward towards the curtain partition before Mr Hardcastle could blink. With an, 'I'll just check your stock, Mr Hardcastle, to save you time as you serve your customer,' I marched through into the area behind the curtains. Despite a muffled shout from the owner I didn't stop and I found myself in a small, furnished room – but it wasn't the stockroom. Immediately before me was a tin bath filled with steaming, soapy water, adjacent to a blazing coal fire. Languishing in the tub was the large naked form of Mrs Hardcastle! I had inadvertently entered the small private living room of the house. With a shriek and a grab for a towel, the cetacean Mrs H. endeavoured to cover her structure. Before I had time to say 'Oops!' I was lifted bodily from behind, catapulted through the store and slung unceremoniously onto the cobbled street outside the shop, much to the alarm and amusement of passers-by. I then narrowly avoided a flying missile coming towards my head – my sample bag – and, fearing for my future welfare, I never ventured near the store again: a bruising defeat in more ways than one!

So, red with embarrassment, I jumped into my car and drove off at a rate of knots in high dudgeon towards my next selling call. But, in my haste to escape from my mortifying experience, I misjudged the speed of an oncoming automobile at a crossroads just outside of the town, cutting across the vehicle and narrowly avoiding a collision. The following half hour or so was to develop into pure motoring farce as the obviously irate other driver screeched to a halt and, to my astonishment, reversed his car (a bright red Austin Ten) onto the grass verge and set off ominously after me in hot pursuit – all the while sounding his horn continuously! Emotionally roiled, I decided rather foolishly to try and outrun him – big mistake.

The day was lovely and sunny, with good dry road surface conditions, so I confidently moved swiftly through the gears and accelerated away to place some distance between our two vehicles. The density of traffic on the North Yorkshire country roads was minimal as I negotiated the sharp bend on the outskirts of the village where, coincidentally, my next scheduled selling call was located. Seeing that the image of the chasing red Austin had yet to appear in my rear-view mirror, I decided to veer off the main road and down a small country lane, reducing my rate of progress in anticipation that my antagonist would continue his pursuit straight through the village and over the horizon – big mistake number two. As I looked for a turning to take me back into the village, I became aware of flashing lights and a red car tailgating my vehicle, the agitated occupant gesticulating towards me with a pointed finger (or was it a closed fist?). Alarmed, I decided not to hang around to find out and accelerated down the narrow country lane once more in an attempt to lose my tenacious pursuer. I began to panic slightly and, deep down being a coward (despite my prowess on the rugby field), I had no intention of having a confrontation with the angry driver, whose bulky figure hunched over the steering wheel seemed to take on more and more menacing and indeed massive physical proportions.

The next thirty minutes passed like a dreadful nightmare as I scorched through the network of tiny country lanes with no planned destination, hoping desperately that the hunter would eventually tire of the chase and let the quarry escape. Eventually we appeared miraculously at a junction with the main road and as I decelerated to negotiate the change in direction I noticed a signpost indicating the mileage to the town of Penrith: we were nearly in the Lake District and some forty miles from my planned work area. With every minute, we were moving further and further away from my sales section.

Racing towards the outskirts of the next village, I was dripping in sweat and beginning to feel nauseous with panic. This, combined with the huge level of concentration and driving skills necessary to keep the car on the road, made me decide that enough was enough. Such a ludicrous theatre of 'car rage' had to be terminated irrespective of whether I was about to be in all probability physically assaulted. Accordingly I slowed down, opened the driver's window and, indicating my 'defeat' with a slowdown signal and a reluctant thumbs-up, brought the automobile to a halt in a lay-by. Opening the car door I stepped out apprehensively into the warm sunlit day. The driver of the bright red Austin Ten brought his vehicle to a halt just a few yards away and slowly emerged from his car. He was indeed the Goliath I had envisaged during our frenetic chase: in fact he was the classic back-row rugby forward, built like the proverbial 'brick shithouse' and literally blocking the sun behind him as he strode towards me.

I decided to take the initiative immediately and, with a smile, advanced slowly forward, proffered a handshake and greeted him as if a long-lost chum. 'Bloody hell! It's not you,' I lied. 'All along I thought you were an old rugby club chum of mine playing "Cops and Robbers" with me,' I explained. I then fabricated that not only was his appearance similar to my rugby-playing mate's, but that he also owned an identical car in make and colour. The deception seemed to work for, on enquiring which rugby club I played for, he immediately placed his massive hand on my shoulder and confirmed that he was a similar sportsman and, as luck would have it, the team he played for had thrashed my club to a heavy defeat earlier in the season!

Following a friendly chat we parted kindred spirits, and agreed to down a few beers on the next return fixture between our respective clubs. Never before had I been so glad that my philosophy of 'consultation before confrontation' had worked – in fact, I had escaped without any mention of the 'crossroads' driving incident, now some distant forty miles away!

High Noon

CHAPTER TEN

Duel

Just over twelve months had elapsed since my introduction into the 'Soapy Business'. Perhaps reflecting on my success in increasing the Company's overall business, I was transferred to another sales area, which according to my area manager had greater volume potential My new sales territory was in direct contrast to the rural and farming communities I had left behind, and included my birthplace Blaydon-on-Tyne. I settled into my new routine quickly, assisted considerably by the fact that I was able to return to my parents' home, with its attendant home comforts, at a much reduced rental.

My mother was delighted to have me back home again, not just for the additional revenue which came in very handy, but also for my companionship, as my sister Joan had married and moved with her husband to a village six miles away. On my return I was given my old bedroom back and this meant my younger brother Gordon was relegated to his former smaller room (which he accepted gracefully, despite having to transfer all his musical instruments and equipment). Gordon was an exceptionally talented musician (indeed, Joan was a wonderful true soprano) and as a young child had quickly mastered the accordion – taught by our father, who had taught himself not only this instrument but also the piano as well. However, much to our father's chagrin, Gordon abandoned the accordion at the age of fifteen for the traditional jazz trombone.

So, now that I was a significant wage earner (as I saw it), I was able to assist my brother in his musical ambitions. This help took the form of his sixteenth birthday present – a much discussed subject – which we bought at Windows, a music shop located in the small shopping arcade at the top of Grainger Street, next to Grey's Monument. Here, we were served by Ronnie Maclean, a well-known local traditional jazz trombonist and, following his expert advice, bought a trombone for the princely sum of twenty-five pounds – making a large hole in my Thomas Hedley weekly salary. Of all the things I was to spend my salary on, the trombone turned out to be one of my best investments: to the discomfort of our neighbours, Gordon practised every evening and, over the last forty years, has given immense pleasure to thousands of traditional jazz fans throughout the North East with his ensemble, The River City Jazz Men.

Still, a more immediate consequence of working for Thomas Hedley in my new sales section was that though it was much smaller geographically, it had a greater density of retail and wholesale outlets. This then was a challenge of a different order – one that I faced with relish. Following several weeks of familiarisation and adjustment, I – and the Company – began to see increased benefits from my semi-confrontational and dramatic style of selling (a style that seemed to work just as well in these more industrialised areas as it had in my previous rural territory). Despite this, however, I was to find that all was not well in my sales sector.

One late Friday afternoon as I drove home on completing my day's work, I went to purchase some chocolate from a grocery store where only three days previously I had negotiated a large volume order. Prior to leaving the shop I had erected an impressive display of merchandise, supported with several point-of-purchase display cards and pricing tickets. It is always to the salesman's advantage to be able to leave evidence of his visit via an erected floor display of merchandise (and this is an integral part of the salesman's in-store operation, which should ideally be located adjacent to the serving counter). Therefore, imagine my surprise and chagrin when, on entering the store, there was no evidence of my previous merchandising labours. According to the staff, the Lever Brothers company rep had called the day before and had dismantled my product display, returned the merchandise to the stockroom and replaced my efforts with a large Persil display!

I was soon to discover over the following weeks that it was common practice for this specific salesman to remove any displayed competitive brands, often without the sanction of the store staff. This was my first introduction to a 'turf war' between Procter & Gamble and their despised competitor Unilever, which was to last at all levels of selling throughout my entire career in the soap industry. I quickly decided to gain my revenge and attempt to correct this unfair activity on my sales patch!

Generally speaking, the store manager would give us reps carte blanche to display his stock, as it was in his interests to be able to generate the extra sales most separate displays produced. So, throughout the next few weeks, whenever I came across a display erected by my rival, down it came; removed to the stockroom and replaced with my own merchandise. Strangely enough, over this period of time our paths never crossed and I had no idea what my enemy looked like. However, I sensed a *High Noon* shoot-out confrontation was imminent.

One damp, miserable morning in the small town of Prudhoe, I parked my car at the top of the main road, which ran through the centre of the village, and set off on foot towards my first retail customer of the day. Arriving at the planned call, I observed through the shop window a rep in negotiation with the owner, with his back towards the entrance. It was commonly accepted that a fellow salesman did not enter a store if there was another one on the premises, thereby avoiding interrupting the flow of the first salesman's operation. So, intending to walk to my next customer, I casually glanced into the parked car outside the store, and I saw that the rear seat was crammed with various items of display material and cartons of product, all highlighting the dreaded brand name of Persil; the enemy was in our midst! Realising that the driver of the car and the rep inside the shop were one and the same, I noticed that he had inadvertently neglected to remove the car's ignition keys. I could not resist the temptation. Quietly slipping into the vehicle, I proceeded to drive the car slowly down the main street and around the corner of the shop parade, parking in a cul-de-sac. I then returned to my vehicle, which was just further up the road from the 'occupied' shop and settled down to watch the anticipated drama develop.

After about ten minutes, the enemy appeared – a tall, military-looking type, complete with trench coat, trilby hat and the traditional leather sample bag. He exited the store with a cheery farewell salute and still looking sideways into the shop, instinctively reached for the non-existent driver's car door. Thunderstruck! My panic-stricken rival, realising the disappearance of his vehicle, looked up and down the thoroughfare several times, becoming more and more agitated, before finally rushing down the road towards a telephone kiosk. I decided to leave the scene of the pantomime I had just engineered and, as I cruised past the distraught occupant of the telephone box, I was curious to learn how the next stage of events would unfold.

The following day I resumed my normal journey plan into Prudhoe. On concluding my sales call at the store where I had last seen my rival, I gathered from the staff that the Unilever rep had summoned the local constabulary and, on locating the 'missing' car minutes later, had been severely ticked off by the law for wasting valuable police time. He was even told that he would be reported to his company.

I felt somewhat guilty on hearing this and even more so when several weeks later, whilst enjoying an early morning breakfast in the local transport café, in walked the 'Persil' man, complete with trench coat, brown trilby and leather sample bag. Carrying his steaming mug of tea, he promptly deposited himself at my table with a cheery, 'I hope you don't mind', and began a pleasant conversation ranging from the weather to the weekend of rugby he was looking forward to. Eventually we exchanged our employers' identities and before we left the café had agreed on a truce to our on-going in-store display battles, even shaking hands on leaving. He never once mentioned the incident of his disappearing automobile, much to my relief.

Many years later our paths crossed once more in London at a retail trade conference where, over a chat at the hotel bar, I owned up to the car disappearance episode in Prudhoe. He smiled benignly at my confession to confirm that he had always regarded me as the main suspect. Luckily for me, however, every time my rival had come across my company car, my ignition keys had never been on display!

The Parting of the Waves

CHAPTER ELEVEN

The Rugby Dance

One of the key benefits following the achievement of my successful entry into the world of selling was undoubtedly the usage of the company motorcar. The instant transition from the pedestrian dependent on public transport to the freedom and independence of the motorist elevated my social standing within my home town of Blaydon-on-Tyne, where an automobile parked down the sloping terraced streets caused great interest among the neighbours and particularly the local kids (who, more used to a procession of tradesmen's commercial conveyances that were horse-drawn, frequently surrounded my car as if it were a vehicle from outer space). Another advantage to having a company car was that my opportunities to attract and snare a higher volume of the opposite sex were increased. Anxious to arrive home from the local dance in presentable and dry circumstances, I found that many ladies were invariably influenced on a rainy Saturday evening by the attractions of the car owner rather than the handsome-looking but pedestrian Adonis queuing for the number 66 bus! It was therefore with some satisfaction, and much to the envy of my team-mates, that I could arrive by car at my rugby club's main annual celebratory function, where in previous years

I had been resigned to walking laboriously up the steep incline of Blaydon Bank to reach the venue.

The rugby club's major annual buffet-and-dance was, undoubtedly, the biggest social highlight of the year in the district, and it always took place at the Miners' Welfare Hall. The event commenced at around 7 p.m. and the decanting of revellers at midnight signalled the end of the festivities. I have yet to witness since such frenetic and wild drinking scenes, which would have rivalled a Klondike Wild West saloon full of thirsty gold prospectors.

Towards the end of the evening, the overheated dance hall was awash with beer, sweat, vomit and discarded items of clothing such as jackets, ties and cardigans. The cacophony of noise reverberated throughout the building, virtually drowning out all conversation as well as the efforts of the resident band who, in attempting to cope with the mayhem surrounding them, appeared to be giving their impression of the last heroic hours on board the *Titanic*!

Attending the function was one of the rugby club's former captains – the formidable 'Panky Holliday', a monster twenty-stone back-row forward, who had led the club with great local success for over ten years. This goliath was capable of prodigious feats of strength and had a reputation for taking no prisoners on the field of play. He was also able to consume gallons of beer during a one-night session, as well as whatever other alcoholic beverages were offered to him in a glass. Towards the end of the evening, feeling the urge to visit the dance hall's facilities, Panky rose unsteadily to his feet and, with glazed eyes, lurched from the table covered with dozens of glasses, bottles, jugs and empty food tureens. Accompanied by some awesome, thunderous belching, which reverberated across the dance hall, he pointed his massive frame in the direction of the gents' and set forth like a lumbering armoured tank, causing the crowded floor to split open like the biblical Red Sea. An uncanny hush descended on the proceedings as it became clear to the enthralled gathering that, not unlike an overfed chameleon, the countenance of the unfortunate Panky was slowly changing from a healthy ruddy complexion to an ominous sickly grey. Faltering in his gait and clutching his large stomach, it became increasingly obvious that he was not going to make the sanctuary of the toilets, and with one mighty heave he emptied the contents of his stomach across the dance-room floor.

The horrified onlookers gasped, and fleeing from the oncoming wave were, however, transfixed by the emergence of an intact meat pie, which appeared to slalom across the glistening floor; its original pastry crimping still evident! To sate his hunger, Panky must have swallowed it whole as if it were a chocolate Smartie. Following a break in the evening's entertainment to allow the resident caretaker time to mop up, the music continued with a somewhat more wary and restrained clutch of dancers, who were having great difficulty in recapturing their former jollity as they stepped and slid their way across the damp floorboards amidst the urinal fragrant atmosphere of Domestos and Dettol. Meanwhile the unfortunate Panky had returned to the bar and catering area and was last seen filling the void in his stomach with a large plate of mixed sandwiches!

The evening finally came to a close with the traditional slow-tempo last waltz. This signalled to the majority of the inebriated male revellers that it was now their last opportunity to click with a member of the opposite sex and hopefully persuade their chosen lady to accept an invitation to walk her home. The overcrowded dance floor soon resembled a mass scrum, with my fellow rugby team colleagues attempting with little success to synchronise their feet movements to the slow rhythm of the Viennese waltz. Their collective failure to manoeuvre their unlucky partners in the correct manner around the dance floor was in sharp contrast to their usual agility and balletic ability to deftly sidestep an opponent on the field of play on a Saturday afternoon.

Don Craven (a handsome wing three-quarter) was, like myself, one of the few members of the club possessing an automobile. He approached me at the bar and, pointing towards two attractive girls entering the cloakroom, indicated that he had been successful in persuading them to accept a lift but, so as not to cramp his style, asked whether I would offer to transport one of the sisters home, albeit to the same residence. I readily agreed. The two ladies lived only a couple of miles away in the small village of Winlaton, which was accessed via a steep winding road and whose inhabitants looked out over the Tyne valley and eastwards towards the city of Newcastle.

Following a quick kiss and cuddle in our respective cars, we bade farewell to the sisters and pointed our vehicles homeward towards Blaydon. With the traditional 'Le Mans' racing start, my team-mate and I sprinted to our automobiles and propelled ourselves through the empty streets of the village and down the steep incline into Blaydon. Unhappily, my car never made it into the town below. Midway down Blaydon Bank I overtook my rival and failed to negotiate the sharp bend exactly opposite the very building where, only one hour previously, we had been celebrating and enjoying ourselves – the Miners' Welfare Hall.

My car proceeded to demolish the nearby bus shelter and, colliding with a gas streetlight standard, shuddered to a stop, the metal pole coming to rest only inches from the car's windscreen. Miraculously, I emerged from the total wreckage unscathed and was immediately collected by my team-mate (following at a less frenetic pace). I was then taken to his nearby home to sober up with many cups of strong coffee. After about an hour following the crash, we made our tentative way to the town police station to report the accident, feeling extremely apprehensive of the outcome (even though it was in the pre-breathalyser era). As we stepped nervously into the foyer of the precinct, a wave of laughter and merriment greeted us. Fortuitously, the two nightshift constables on duty happened to be fellow rugby team-mates, whom we had been sharing a few beers with only a couple of hours ago!

Taking a deep breath, I attempted to explain the circumstances of my accident (I swerved to avoid a fox!) as Tom Baker, the jovial station sergeant, invited us into his office. Ignoring my plight, he extracted a bottle from his desk and offered us a tot of whisky – to calm our nerves! We dared not refuse, hoping that the pints of recently consumed coffee would help dilute the Scotch. On establishing that no one else was involved in the crash and that I was not suffering from any injury, and seeing no reason to take the matter any further, Sergeant Baker telephoned the Gas Board to report the damaged streetlight. Then he offered us a nightcap and, with a knowing smile, bade us goodnight, with a reminder not to be late for rugby training on Tuesday (the Sergeant was our club captain). My companion and I left the station heaving a sigh of relief, hardly believing my good fortune. However, would I be so fortunate when I presented the bad news to Thomas Hedley & Co. senior management on the following Monday morning?

With trepidation I telephoned the Newcastle-based District Sales Office early the next Monday to report my weekend misfortune. I was instructed to report forthwith for a meeting with my formidable northern district sales manager, Jack Caygill. I could still vividly recall that at the commencement of my career he had warmly welcomed me into the Company, whilst at the same time firing my (then) immediate boss. Arriving in good time at the District Sales Office for my confrontation with the legendary J.W. and feeling absolutely miserable and contrite, I was totally resigned to an ignominious exit from the Company – receiving my P45 and the traditional J.W. boot up the backside. I feared I was destined to begin my life all over again: queuing for the Venture Bus, cadging a lift on my brother-in-law's motorcycle and, worst of all, explaining to the delicious Judy, whom I had just met, that our assignation for a romantic dinner at the Duke of Wellington in Riding Mill that weekend would have to be cancelled due to lack of transport. Oh! Death, where is thy sting!

On entering the office I received a wry smile from Mary – J.W.'s personal secretary – and was asked to enter his office immediately. Pausing only to knock on the door to announce my arrival, I once again found myself in the presence of the great man. His appearance had not really altered since my last visit to his sanctum well over twelve months previously and his loud-checked suit was shrouded in a fog of Woodbine fumes.

J.W. beckoned me forward to the front of his huge desk. With a fierce stare, he addressed me as I remained standing, like a headmaster admonishing one of his pupils: 'Whatever you have to say lad, no matter what excuse, in totally writing off hundreds of pounds of Company automobile equipment, you've just cost this sales district not just a tidy amount of money, but you're also jeopardising the lifeblood of this company, and that's business!' At this juncture the pitch of his voice rose angrily. 'Instead of farting around in my office, you should be out there now, hammering competition and selling our goods to keep our factories ticking over! Since you joined us just over a year ago, you've made good progress and I see that you're starting to win a few of our sales competitions, but you can only make progress in this company if you keep your nose clean, and that means handling Company equipment responsibly and proving that your personal conduct and sales performance is head and shoulders above that of all your fellow colleagues. I'm going to give you one last chance to stay on board and it's up to you to grasp it!' he concluded, giving me a hard glare. Still, my heart soared – a reprieve, a second chance; perhaps my weekend evening with the delectable Judy was back on track!

My thoughts were rudely interrupted, however, when J.W. outlined the task he was setting me to justify my last chance. 'The spare Company vehicle is parked at the rear of the office and here are the keys, but the key to you staying with my organisation is that I want you to sell the entire residual stock of a line we're discontinuing – namely Gleem Toothpaste – in addition to you maintaining your sales impetus of our ongoing range of brands. We've a total of five hundred cases of toothpaste collecting dust on the factory floor and you personally have four weeks to clear the stock.'

Some years prior to my arrival, Thomas Hedley & Co. had decided to test-market a dentifrice product. However, mainly due to the fact that major distribution of PCPs (Personal Care Products, which included toothpastes) was in the domain of retail pharmacy outlets rather than retail grocery stores, the launch had been an unmitigated failure – the T. Hedley brand strengths were undoubtedly in the grocery sector of the trade; a sector which was unwilling to entertain new product categories such as PCP merchandise. Nevertheless, the gauntlet had been thrown down and as I left the Sales Office I was determined to meet the challenge. I was especially motivated by the gift of another automobile and the prospect of keeping my date on Saturday evening with the lovely Judy. I set to considering seriously which of my retail grocery customers would accept the unlikely, previously non-stocked product of toothpaste.

So, after a restless night's sleep dreaming of endless tubes of toothpaste leaping over stiles, I emerged from my home the following morning apprehensive but determined in my sales ability to successfully clear the Company's residual quantities of what I euphemistically christened 'Gloom Toothpaste'. My pet name for the dentifrice product reflected my pessimism and real concern over whether or not I would be successful in the task ahead of me during the next few weeks. Added to this was the stress of the uncertainty of my sales career, which was hanging over me like the Sword of Damocles. During my planning and preparation the night before, I had calculated that in the remaining available four-week selling period, and with nearly two hundred retail customers located across my sales section, my objective – to keep my job – could only be achieved by clearing the five-hundred-case allocation of Gloom Toothpaste at an average of twenty-five cases per day, equivalent to 2.5 cases per retail outlet. With every refusal to purchase, the volume target per store would increase accordingly.

As I walked down Church Street in Blaydon towards my first morning call, Jack Caygill's stentorian 'last-chance saloon' ultimatum echoed in my head and I quickened my step anxiously towards my destination. After the first few selling calls I knew I was in trouble. Despite launching into my finest Shakespearean dramatic presentations, I was frustratingly unable to persuade the man in the brown coat to purchase even one tube of Gloom, never mind the minimum quota of one outer case containing twenty-four units of large-sized toothpaste. The grocer was unwilling to invest in a product that had ostensibly been discontinued from the market, was receiving no advertising or promotional support and was a line of merchandise which he preferred to leave to the retail chemist and the chain stores such as F.W. Woolworths. Plan A was failing.

Shaken, but still determined, I resorted to Plan B, which was to approach the sector of the trade that dominated the dentifrice market: the retail chemist – a group of outlets which I had hitherto no knowledge of and which at that specific time had no direct trading links with my company. It was at one of our unit sales meetings, I recalled, that a senior salesman colleague – Billy Hinckley – had confirmed that, several years ago, pharmacists had never forgiven T. Hedley & Co. for attempting to introduce a toothpaste product into the grocery trade (considering, as they did, that this line of PCP merchandise was traditionally in the purview of the chemist). This had resulted in a subsequent broad-scale damaging embargo on any merchandise manufactured by T.H., and as a direct result had contributed to the unmitigated and costly failure of my company's UK dentifrice test-market.

With this appalling background knowledge in mind, I approached the first of two pharmacies located in Blaydon with some apprehension, hoping that as a local lad I would receive a friendly welcome. The first call was at the oldest established chemist outlet in town, which had been in the same family for centuries. As I arrived at 'Cuby's the Chemist', I could see that the shop window was sparsely filled with dust-covered dummy cartons and empty bottles, attracting little interest from passers-by. The last time I had been in the shop was when I was a young lad on an errand for my grandmother's prescription, and to purchase some liquorice root and cinnamon sticks (the latter I smoked in the graveyard at the rear of St Cuthbert's Church, just further up the street, and was caught by the curate, who admonished me severely).

Despite this nostalgia, I focused on the task ahead. I entered the store and it was as if I had stepped back into a locked medieval time capsule. The inside of the shop was gloomy and poorly lit: the walls, floor and ceiling were painted in a dark funereal grey. Along the entire nearest wall were rows and rows of shelves supporting dark mahogany boxes, each one labelled by some long-gone sign writer in spidery handwritten gold letters which indicated their contents, such as Lint, Sulphur and Linctus. The only splash of colour in the entire shop was a row of large, ornately shaped apothecary jars, filled with bilious green, purple and yellow liquids which would not have looked out of place in Merlin's ancient abode. Welcome to the fifteenth century! I had a sinking feeling that any slick point-of-purchase sales presentation of the twentieth century would not be successful. Mistress Cuby, a thin gaunt woman who needed to shave, shuffled to the tiny serving counter and in a squeaky voice enquired my business. On hearing my proposition, she pointed to the top shelf immediately behind her to indicate four boxes of Gleem Toothpaste, covered in dust, and which must have been at least three to four years old. Following this came a request for me to uplift the discontinued stock! I diverted her attention immediately from my predicament by requesting to purchase some liquorice root and cinnamon sticks and, after hurriedly paying for them, pocketed my schoolboy treats and fled the premises.

On entering the Roberts Pharmacy, the remaining retail chemist outlet further up Church Street, I was met with even sterner resistance from the owner. Once he had learnt that I represented Thomas Hedley & Co., he courteously showed me the door, indicating his disapproval of my organisation ever since the Company's original attempt to break into the UK dentifrice market via the grocery trade. He vociferously refused to accept any proposition linked to Gleem Toothpaste, and thus emphasised the ongoing grudge held against Thomas Hedley & Co. by the general pharmacist.

Survival Plans A and B were now dead ducks. I retreated to my car slowly, and glumly opened the boot lid to deposit my various bits of selling equipment. It was then that I noticed a couple of golf balls in the boot, which had dropped out of my golf bag the previous evening when I had unpacked this equipment from the car. The golf balls immediately gave me an idea for Plan C – and with it the realisation that I could dismiss the retail chemist and concentrate on the retail grocer once more.

Over the last momentous year, I had observed that the grocer was, with few exceptions, always on the lookout for bargains, free samples and cash-bonus buying incentives, etc. In a flash of inspiration I decided to introduce a 'trade lottery': a purchasing incentive for the grocer to buy Gloom Toothpaste. I would use my brand new golfing equipment (which I had won in a previous month's District Sales Competition) as the first prize. Aware that many of my retail customers were members of the local grocers' Golfing Society, I was hopeful that the first prize would be a strong incentive for them to participate in my lottery. Despite my own enthusiasm for the sport, it made sense to trade in the expensive sports gear so that I could salvage my career. After all, if I were successful in saving my job, there would surely be other opportunities and sales competitions where I could win another set of golf clubs.

The structure of my trade competition was simple: for every case of Gloom purchased by the grocer, he would receive a numbered ticket; for each case ordered in excess of four cases, he would receive an extra two lottery tickets. Following the end of the sales period, all the tickets would be placed in a hat and the winning number drawn by an independent member of the public (me!).

Fired with new enthusiasm, and armed with my shining bag of golfing equipment (in pristine condition) and a couple of books of lottery tickets, I set forth the following morning feeling positive and optimistic for the first time since my auto accident. My self-confidence was not misplaced: by lugging the first prize into every retail outlet as a centrepiece of my presentation, the orders rolled in. Within two further weeks of sales calls I had cleared my entire allocation of toothpaste (which I had reverted to calling Gleem to match the grin on my face when I telephoned my District Sales Office to confirm my sales success). The following evening I received a telephone call from my leader, J.W. Caygill, confirming my job security and congratulating me on my sales performance. He ended the call with: 'Any further auto accidents and there's no second chance.'

For the record, I duly conducted the lottery draw at the end of the month and presented the first prize to the winner: a Mrs Robinson, owner of the village grocery store in Ryton, a small hamlet on the banks of the Tyne. Fortunately, Mrs R. did not play golf and I was able to purchase the equipment back from her at a knockdown price. My toast had fallen butter side up; my career and golf course activity were back on track!

Inconvenience!

CHAPTER TWELVE

Caught Short

One of the problems often facing 'salesmen of the road' is not being blessed with the facilities the traditional office worker takes for granted – namely the toilet! All human beings need to evacuate their bladder and bowels, generally on a daily basis, and the rep is no exception, but how and where he can perform this bodily need is often up to his ingenuity and spontaneous initiative. Generally speaking, the shopkeeper will often oblige and allow the 'bursting' salesman the use of his store's facilities, usually located at the rear of the premises. However, when working in the middle of a rural area the salesman can often find himself in need of a toilet between selling calls. Then the unfortunate man has to link up with the sheep and cattle in a field and go behind a hedge or large oak tree to avoid what is euphemistically called 'being caught short'!

However, one of the benefits of being a salesman of the road is the wonderful, often unsupervised freedom he enjoys, particularly when, with the car window down and breathing in the healthy countryside air, he can stop anywhere he decides and choose from numerous spectacular rural locations to enjoy an isolated picnic-type lunch. It was just before leaving the small town of Middleton in Teesdale, at around 1 p.m., that I took advantage of this perk by purchasing from the local Cooperative grocery store a delicious pork pie, an apple tart and a bottle of Tizer for my outdoor lunch. I drove a few miles from the town and, parking in a lay-by, collected my picnic lunch from the car seat, leapt over the nearby fence and sat on the grassy banks of the River Tees, which slowly meandered just past the lay-by. Although the large pork pie would have been sufficient for at least two people, I was ravenous. I easily managed to scoff the entire meat pastry and the apple tart, and washed them down with the effervescent cordial.

Three hours later, on finishing my final selling call of the day, I was commencing my journey home when I felt the compelling call of Mother Nature. Unfortunately I was several miles from the nearest town (and therefore the closest toilets), and it was beginning to rain quite heavily. Fearing that I might be caught short, I was relieved when, as luck would have it, I noticed a large commercial building ahead of me. This turned out to be the regional offices and warehouse administration headquarters of the National Milk Marketing Board. Parking my car quickly in the visitors' car park, I sprinted desperately to the entrance and into the reception area. I managed to persuade the lady at the desk to allow me the use of their facilities and hurriedly made my way to the men's staff toilet (which was located on the third floor of the office complex and certainly much more preferable than squatting behind a hedge in a rain-lashed field).

Arriving somewhat breathlessly at the door marked 'staff toilets', having dashed up three flights of stairs, I

entered the facilities, switched on the light, locked the
cubicle door behind me and at last relaxed! Ever since
I can recall, I have always followed the same somewhat
idiosyncratic routine when using the 'thunder box':
trousers and pants down, squat, elbows on knees, hands
over eyes and then contemplate! Settling comfortably on
the wooden (oh bliss!) toilet seat, my thoughts travelled
to the weekend ahead and the forthcoming Saturday
evening when I would be escorting the delectable Judy
to the Tynedale Hunt Ball. My concentration was
briefly interrupted only when someone entered to use
the wall-mounted urinal, washed their hands and left,
clashing the door with a bang.

However, when I slowly removed my hands from
my face and opened my eyes, all I was aware of was
an inky pitch-black void! Panicking, I blinked several
times, rubbed my eyes vigorously, but all to no avail:
there was not a chink of light and in my alarm I wildly
concluded that I had been struck blind. Perhaps I was
experiencing some kind of instant, massive, yet painless
optical haemorrhage! Assuming that the fluorescent
strip lighting was still blazing away above me on the
ceiling, I dropped to my bared knees and crawled about
like some demented sightless lunatic for what seemed
like an eternity, before eventually managing to locate
the sliding bolt of the cubicle door. With some difficulty
I was able to open the door and began to shout and
wail continuously, 'Help, someone please help me!' It
seemed to take ages as I slowly inched my way out of
the cubicle and across the central tiled floor area to try
and locate the main bathroom door. Flashing through

my mind were thoughts of guide dogs, white sticks, no more dashing up the green rugby field or looking at the beautiful Judy. My world, within seconds, had been blown apart and I felt tears welling up in my now useless eyes.

Suddenly the bathroom door was flung open and, to my amazement, I was greeted by a dazzling bright shaft of light! I found myself gazing down at a pair of well-polished shoes, whose owner had switched on the toilet lights and, with a horrified distasteful look on his face, exclaimed, 'What on earth are you doing? Disgraceful!' to the semi-naked person grovelling on the floor below him. In my sheer panic, I had neglected to hitch up and rearrange my errant trousers and Y-fronts. As a result, the owner of the polished shoes was now gazing down on my well-muscled but naked backside. To me, however, it was a miracle and, ignoring my semi-nudity, I clasped my saviour around his ankles and thanked him profusely – I had after all been totally blind and now I could see again – 'Praise the Lord!'

What I hadn't remembered in my panic was that, at around that time, the UK was in the grip of mass industrial unrest, which culminated in the Government introducing a four-day-week in an attempt to conserve nationwide energy. As a direct result of this action the population had been subject to random electricity cuts and the inevitable consequent hardships and inconveniences. The explanation for my temporary blindness was not after all a sudden optical haemorrhage, but the result of an employee of the Milk Marketing Board who had used the urinal whilst

I was still 'involved' in the adjoining cubicle, and then adhered commendably to the notice pasted to the tiled toilet wall, 'Save Energy! Switch off!' – and had duly done so! My dilemma had been compounded twofold, however, by the fact that I had not heard the click of the light switch on the employee's exit, and that the toilet facilities I was using were located in the centre of the building and were therefore devoid of windows and any natural light.

Since that day, whenever I receive a regular charity request for a donation to the disabled blind movement, I find that I feel compelled to oblige. However, I must confess that whatever contribution I do make is not for any altruistic reason, but as a direct result of my experience in the gents' toilets of the Milk Marketing Board and my brief, but nevertheless terrifying, entry into the tragic world of blindness.

The Clinic

CHAPTER THIRTEEN

Eccentricities

One of the benefits not often appreciated by the younger salesman (particularly in the early stages of his career) is the valuable experience and priceless knowledge that can be gleaned from his observation of, and encounters with, the retail grocer. There is no question that during my first few years in retail selling I must have witnessed countless examples of the triangular traits of the good, the bad and the ugly in the man in the brown coat. It was in observing these characteristics and learning how to handle them, that I discovered they had rubbed off onto my psyche as well, enabling me hopefully to become a more mature and adroit person in the handling of people. More importantly to my career, however, those early day-to-day in-store selling experiences and confrontations contributed enormously to my successful climb up the P&G management ladder. Yet, along the way, there were certain challenging situations within the grocery trade that often left me confused and, indeed, occasionally alarmed. Take 'Tarquin' and 'Billy Webster' for example . . .

It was December 1959. Having survived the first two years in the gladiatorial and competitive arena of Salesman versus Grocer, I still found myself relishing the cut and thrust of the constant battle of the often abrasive protracted in-store negotiations. Frequently I would find myself trying to reach an agreement over a minimum order, valued at only a few pounds but taking over half an hour to close, whilst later in the day in a similar-sized store it would take me less than five minutes to agree an order for merchandise worth hundreds of pounds. A time-and-motion study analyst would have had a great report to submit.

Around that time, one late Friday afternoon, I arrived in the village of Stocksfield and parked outside my final call of the day, Mr Patterson's combined Grocery and Post Office emporium. As I entered the store, I sensed immediately that there was something different about the interior of the shop from my previous visits. Whereas before I could recall that the layout of the store had been haphazard, with merchandise piled higgledy-piggledy in various clumps across the counters and restricted floor area, I now saw before me strong evidence of a definite feminine touch. Instead of a chaotic mess, there were methodically stacked groups of grocery products highlighted with brightly coloured price tickets written in bold artistic handwriting. The serving counters were polished and in pristine condition and there was an overpowering scent of a fragrant lemon furniture polish.

I was soon to discover the reason for this startling transformation, for appearing headfirst through the floor-hatch opening of the subterranean stockroom was not the rotund figure of Mr Patterson or the anticipated new female assistant, but a middle-aged man with blond hair (a definite toupee!), exuding what I presumed was a powerful exotic aftershave. The newcomer was dressed in quite distinctive, rather Bohemian garb, with a light-blue-striped overall, cream trousers, matching shoes and the whole ensemble was topped off by a jaunty red beret. This unexpected vision could have stepped straight out of *La Cage aux Folles*. On emerging from the floor opening, this man greeted me with an effusive, warm, friendly smile and shook my hand (somewhat effeminately) whilst announcing that his name was Tarquin – the new proprietor.

Apparently, together with a partner, he had just recently purchased the business from Mr P. and had only commenced trading a couple of weeks ago. I congratulated him on his acquisition and reaffirmed that T. Hedley & Co. would give him every assistance so that he could make a success of his business. We then moved on to discuss my company's trading terms and product range, together with the current promotional offers. It was at this juncture that Tarquin reached for my hand and beckoned me towards the open hatch door, suggesting (coyly) that perhaps we could descend into the stockroom to check the store's current inventory of soap powders. Totally preoccupied and focused on the order I anticipated writing, I innocently descended the wooden staircase into the dimly lit stockroom, with the flamboyant shop owner following closely behind me. Climbing down into the semi-darkness, I asked if he would perhaps switch on the cellar lights, but the only response I received was a gentle buffeting from behind, a closing waft of exotic fragrance and a hand softly brushing against my backside! The penny dropped as I realised immediately the dangerous situation I was in. Instinctively changing direction and turning, I brushed past the predatory proprietor, sprinted back up the staircase and, clambering onto the shop floor, shouted, 'Just remembered; have to make a phone call!' With great relief I exited the store quickly and made my escape.

Inside my automobile I chided myself on my naivety in not sensing the signals of the preying male. I later heard on the local reps' grapevine that Messrs Tarquin and Partner's emporium had been named a no-go zone and, not unlike my fellow chums of the road, I never ventured near the store again!

'Billy Webster' was a pleasant enough store manager and ran one of Moores Stores' busy retail-chain grocery outlets, located on Main Street in the industrial iron-and-steel town of Consett. The area was well populated with hundreds of steel workers and their families, but it was an abysmal place to reside in, continually covered in a depressing industrial smog, which often meant that the entire area was enveloped in a sinister thin film of red dust. As a result, the poor housewife constantly fought a lonely hygiene battle against the muck and grime polluting the air, often needing to launder her family's clothes two or three times every week. Needless to say, the town of Consett was a godsend for the soap manufacturer and, indeed, represented nearly thirty per cent of my section's total business.

After meeting with Billy Webster a couple of times, I soon established that he had a problem: he thought he suffered from continuous life-threatening medical problems and that he didn't have long for this world. It became apparent quickly that he was just waiting for the undertaker to measure him up and, despite his frequent trips to his GP and visits to a various array of medical consultants (who all deemed his imminent demise unlikely), he remained convinced that his death was just around the corner. So much taken up was he with his health problems that I soon discovered the only way I could get him to focus on my business presentation fully was for me to adopt the role of a sympathetic doctor, and in between his self-diagnostic malady analysis, I was able to sneak in my suggested product order. Eventually I became quite adept at playing the dual role of salesman and the acquiescing General Practitioner.

On each month's visit Mr Webster greeted me with a different illness, ranging from the commencement of leprosy (it turned out to be a small common boil) to ulcers (a mild tummy upset) and on my most recent visit he had been convinced he had elephantiasis, which turned out to be a slightly swollen ankle. With such an obsession, Billy Webster's store office resembled a well-stocked first-aid clinic. Rows and rows of various-coloured medicine bottles filled the shelves; cartons of pills and lozenges were on every surface; several inhalers and syringes were scattered about the room; even a set of stethoscopes was hanging on the hook behind the door.

That day, my early morning call to Moores Stores coincided with the beginning of a major Company merchandising blitz designed to persuade every retail grocer to allow a major in-store floor display of T. Hedley brands. To motivate its salesmen fully, the Company was offering an attractive first prize in a Display Competition – a weekend in Paris for two, all expenses paid. Already my imagination was running wild: a weekend in Paris with the delectable Judy – utter bliss! I just had to be the victor of this competition.

Accordingly, I decided to embark upon creating a series of innovative in-store displays across my sales section, each supported with a different theme. In the case of Billy Webster's store, I decided that the most successful display would be one that indirectly mirrored some of the everyday housewife's on-going domestic 'medical' problems; a 'laundry clinic' as it were, where the housewife would be offered the full range of T. Hedley brands together with advice on how our cleaning products could solve their washday blues. 'Softer Hands – Get Rid of Chilblains with

Mild Fairy Soap' and 'Try Flash and Eliminate Backaches with the Once Over Household Cleaner – No Messy Suds, No Wiping Dry' were just some of the medical solutions on display, as were dozens of specifically printed cards highlighting the special in-store competitive pricing.

The display proved to be a huge hit. Billy Webster was in his element, subconsciously identifying himself with the medical theme and enthusiastically supporting the mass display of our merchandise throughout the shop. He even joined in the thematic fun of the merchandising activity, wandering around his store in a white coat with his beloved set of stethoscopes dangling around his neck. In fact, the display was such a success that it played a major part in my winning the much-desired first prize!

With much to thank Billy Webster for (Judy, me, Paris, ooh la la!), I happily carried out my normal routine of checking the distribution of Thomas Hedley products in the store on my next visit. However, when I entered the manager's 'clinic', it was to find Mr Webster sprawled in his chair, munching a huge meat pie and looking somewhat disconsolate. Asking me to take the seat next to him, he announced mournfully that he had just made out his last will and testament – his current malady being life-threatening chronic constipation! Yet, despite this fatal internal condition, Mr Webster still carried on munching his favourite 'Desperate Dan' meat pie, revealing that his illness had been a problem for over two weeks. Commiserating with the afflicted man, I was only sorry that there was no advice in the medical display to help him!

The following month on my next scheduled visit – surprise, surprise! – Billy Webster was still alive and kicking. He greeted me warmly and enthusiastically and confirmed that he was indeed in a sound state of health, although (wait for it!) with the caveat that when he arose that morning he had stubbed his toe on the utensil lurking beneath the bed – perhaps he had fractured it? He then proceeded to remove the appropriate sock and shoe and asked me to examine it. Things never change! And as I write this, I believe that Billy Webster, with his innate powers of recovery, is still going strong. However, I'm convinced that when he does go to that great supermarket in the sky, the local hospitals will reject his body parts for potential transplants: presumably they won't wish to take a chance!

Thirsty Work!

CHAPTER FOURTEEN

Fun and Games

Several miles south of the iron-and-steel sprawling Dante's *Inferno* of Consett was the small mining community of Stanley, whose unfortunate inhabitants also suffered from the fallout of its neighbouring town's industrial pollution. This descended onto their washing lines regularly, especially when the prevailing northerly wind was sweeping vigorously down the terraced streets. The largest retail store in the town was a branch of the F.W. Woolworths organisation or 'Woolies' as it was affectionately known and, like its grocery competitors, it carried out a roaring trade in household laundry and cleaning products. Whilst the store obtained most of its merchandise via the company's central-buying office in its London HQ, T. Hedley & Co. also encouraged its salesmen to visit their local Woolworths periodically in order to actively influence the building of in-store product displays, thereby increasing the throughput of its merchandise into the housewife's basket.

So, following several calls on this outlet, I quickly established a good rapport with not only the store manager but also his number two assistant, who was responsible for all the in-store and window displays. The assistant's name was Jane. She was breathtakingly gorgeous, tall and slim, with auburn hair, a perfect aquiline nose and a ravishing smile. I fell in love, yet again! After several vain attempts to persuade Jane to accompany me on a date, she eventually agreed. Success! That subsequent Saturday evening we travelled into Newcastle to enjoy the theatre and a meal in the Eldon Grill. Heads turned in admiration as we entered the restaurant after the theatre performance, and I felt honoured to be escorting such a stunning lady. However, Jane seemed oblivious that her profile was the focus of so much attention wherever we went; she dismissed all complimentary glances with down-to-earth 'Don't be so daft' asides to me. I was of course delighted to escort her on several other occasions over the next few weeks, yet during this time I couldn't help but notice that her behaviour was sometimes rather odd. Often, when discussing a previous incident or encounter fresh in my mind from a recent evening's date, Jane would frequently look at me with a quizzical and vague expression and abruptly switch the conversation to another topic. I never received an invitation to her home to meet the family and we would always rendezvous outside the Post Office building in the centre of the town, not her residential home. Often some evenings ended with a passionate window-steaming session in my automobile, yet other evenings generated nothing more than a lukewarm perfunctory kiss and a demure smile. I was somewhat puzzled to say the least.

The mystery of this strange behaviour continued until the day I decided to make an unscheduled call at Jane's store, just prior to closing time at around

5 p.m., when I intended to surprise her with my visit and to suggest a quick drink in the local pub before we went our separate ways home. As I parked just outside the rear of Woolies, I saw Jane appear from the staff entrance looking as delectable as ever. Then, to my bewilderment, she was followed immediately by another Jane dressed in an identical tweed coat outfit and a matching tweed hat! I was astonished. I realised I had been presented with what is colloquially known in sales promotion jargon as 'Two for the price of one'! Walking over to them for an explanation, we all ended up going to the Star and Garter public house. There it soon became clear that I had been the innocent victim of the 'Stanley Terrible Twins' – a charade that was ongoing. And, far from being contrite, they offered no apology, appearing to have thoroughly enjoyed the deception!

Following a couple of drinks I found myself able to accept their humorous narrative of our 'threesome' experiences over the last few weeks. I also began to understand their motivation: Jane, the passionate out-going girl (steamy car windows), alternated with June, the quiet and demure sister, who was apparently too coy to accept the advances of would-be suitors and relied upon sharing her sister's conquests. However, there was to be a happy ending to this tale, for a year later I heard that the sisters had met and married identical twin brothers and, I understand, lived happily ever after. I often wondered if the girls employed the same tactics in the early stages of their courtship with their future spouses, or whether the twin brothers eventually won their hearts by beating them at their own game of deception!

Despite such setbacks in my love life, and a succession of short-lived girlfriend relationships, there was one lady who persistently held my regard: the stunning Judy. I had been aware of Judy Falvey's identity – and her apparent penchant for gentlemen escorts and their trademark 'County Set' sports-car lifestyle – for some time, working as she did with my sister Joan at the North Eastern Electricity Authority. However, I first met Judy one Saturday night at the Gosforth Assembly Rooms (or 'GosAss' as it was affectionately known), a local dance hall.

Stumbling onto the dance floor with my Thomas Hedley colleague, John Scott, and a few chums from the rugby fraternity – all much the worse for wear with drink as we had quaffed many pints of the local beer at our respective rugby club bars and were by now in high spirits – I spotted the delectable Judy immediately through the crowd of admirers all presenting themselves to her as candidates for the next dance. With my confidence bolstered by the pints I had drunk, I decided to introduce myself and, breaking through the scrum of eager males, I was able to confront the centre of attraction. Sweating profusely (beer and the central heating) I blurted out: 'You're the girl who drives in fast sports cars!' Withering me with a look, Judy replied, 'And you're not only drunk, but you need a towel!' I was devastated. Why had I said that? I was left looking rather stupid and forlorn and the subsequent butt of my colleagues' irreverent humour. To make events even worse, my chum and fellow soap salesman John Scott 'scored' that very same evening with Kath – a delightful and voluptuous girl from the village of Swalwell (whom he was later to marry after a vigorous courtship).

Over the next week I glumly gave up any chance I might have had with Judy after such a disastrous beginning, even though I couldn't seem to get her out of my mind. However, the next Saturday soon rolled around and I was determined to make up for my poor start by presenting myself to her in the best possible light. I deliberately reduced my intake of the 'amber nectar' during the traditional after-match clubhouse celebrations (despite a resounding victory over our local rivals Ryton RFC), as my sole objective was to be able to show myself as a sober and well-behaved gentleman that evening at the 'GosAss' dance. Alas, despite this strategy the delicious Judy failed to appear at the dance hall and, in my disappointment, I vicariously imagined her enjoying herself at some posh venue with a cavalry-twilled gent in his MGB GT.

So, sod it! With no Judy to impress, I decided to drown my sorrows in the upstairs bar and to the rhythm and beat of the Pete Deucher Jazz Band. And, I have to say, it was not without a Herculean effort that I forgot my quest and began to enjoy myself. Anyway, it was towards the end of the evening that it was established, via the usual hazy alcoholic social grapevine around the bar, that there was an open invitation to a party to celebrate a certain Tom Forster's birthday later that evening. Although my close group of fellow rugby-playing chums and I were not familiar with the birthday boy, an open invitation to further late-evening entertainment was irresistible. Thus, it was not surprising that shortly after the last dance heralded the end of the proceedings, we could be seen grabbing our coats and stumbling into our respective automobiles to head off to the next stage of the evening's entertainment – the birthday party in Wylam, a small village located several miles away, overlooking the River Tyne.

En route to the party I found driving my motor vehicle (my beloved four-seater Ford Popular) especially hard going – indeed, changing gear and steering the car were proving particularly troublesome. However, this was not down to my inebriated state, as may have been expected, but because I was also driving with an additional handicap – that of six extra, strapping passengers!

So, finally arriving at our destination (thankfully all in one piece, which was due more to luck than any skill on my part) and armed with several crates of Newcastle Brown Ale (collected from the bar before we left), we headed for the party at number 19 Tyneview Villas. Crowding the path up to the cottage, we hammered on the front door enthusiastically. In response to our energetic knocking, the door opened slowly to reveal a rather sober-looking, middle-aged chap who, before he could utter a word, was quickly brushed aside by the stampede of the jostling and raucous incoming throng. Careering down the hallway, we soon found ourselves in a small, reasonably well-furnished lounge with a welcoming coal fire, but, to our collective chagrin, there was no evidence of an ongoing party. Indeed, the room had the atmosphere of a doctor's waiting room, with about a dozen sober patients sitting around in various chairs. The only alcohol on offer appeared to be the sherry they were sipping from small coloured glasses.

However, with our entrance, the atmosphere in the room changed dramatically: out came the Newcastle Brown Ale (served in any receptacle that we could lay our hands on, be it cups, vases or even the collection of Toby Jugs from the glass-display cabinet in the corner of the room) and my old mate John Scott (a terrific baritone) immediately launched into a rendering of the famous Northumberland folksong 'Cushie Butterfield' (with the many choruses sung with gusto not only by the 'invaders' but also by the now rejuvenated, astonished 'patients'). Soon the revelry hit an all-new high with the introduction of various rugby 'ditties' and drinking competitions. It didn't take long before everyone was really letting their hair down and thoroughly enjoying themselves.

It was about an hour after our arrival that I decided to call a halt to the proceedings temporarily by asking everyone to raise their glasses (or whatever) to toast the birthday boy, Tom Forster. After my effusive speech, there followed a rather stunned silence, and the middle-aged chap who had been thrust aside as he opened the door on our arrival, announced that the birthday party was not for Tom Forster, but rather for Agnes – a large, red-faced, middle-aged lady, who had been cavorting in the centre of the lounge attempting to squeeze her whale-like torso under a handheld rope as the first contestant in a limbo-dancing contest! We were not, as we had thought, at number 19 Tyneview Villas, but rather at number 9, a few doors down!

Stuttering in my apology, and preparing to decamp from the premises forthwith, our hasty withdrawal was stopped by a hot and flustered Agnes. Clambering onto the creaking dining-room table, she implored us not to desert her in what had become the party of a lifetime. Her appeals touched our hearts and, dismissing Tom Forster without further ado, the party immediately got under way again, its success being later confirmed by a policeman turning up in the early hours of the morning to curtail all the noise and bedlam!

However, after such a memorable party, the following working week was, in contrast, extra dreary. My predicament with Judy came back to haunt me with full force, and I winced over the embarrassment I had made of myself. Still, prepared to be made a fool of yet again,

I decided to repeat my tactics over the coming weekend (less drink, more charm) on the off chance that this time, Judy would definitely make an appearance at the 'GosAss' dance.

So, that Saturday evening, as I was looking around the dance hall, it was with relief and trepidation that I recognised Judy's svelte figure. Dressed in a stunning black outfit, she was surrounded by her usual posse of admirers. This time completely sober, I strode through the pack of eager men, determined not to repeat my experience of two weeks ago. Yet, before I could open my mouth – and perhaps put my foot in it – Judy greeted me with, 'For the record, I don't only go out with men in fast sports cars!' Then, giving me an arch look, she added, 'However, I'm pleased to see you can stand up straight tonight and that you don't need a towel!' followed by a cheeky grin. All was not lost! Salvation! The wonderful Judy had overlooked my previous gaffe and was giving me another chance.

That night I was able to dance with Judy several times – proud to be with the most beautiful woman on the dance floor – and I was thrilled when she accepted my offer of a lift home (albeit in my small 'unsporty' black Ford Popular). And, I must have redeemed myself in Judy's eyes, because from that time on we began to date regularly.

Our subsequent courtship was to prove both fulfilling and challenging – often Judy's flashing eyes would herald a bout of either passion or punch-ups! However, it didn't take long before we settled into a firm relationship and embarked on several terrific holidays together. I'm sure the constant euphoria I felt in those early days would have had me grinning inanely all the time – hopeful as I was that we might become something more permanent (rugby taking second place now that Judy was in my life) – but I was saved from this embarrassing fate by my daily confrontations with the irascible grocer, who made sure my feet stayed firmly on the ground!

Indeed, looking back at that memorable time, it was not just my personal life that was so eventful. My working week still continued to throw up the odd quirky incident – and eccentric character – which managed to catch my otherwise preoccupied attention . . .

It was a late sunny Friday morning, and I was on one of the roads leading to the town of Consett near the village of Blackhill, having already made several selling calls that day. Deciding to take an early lunch, I began to look for somewhere to stop. As I drove, the bright sunshine started to retreat gradually behind the wafting layers of industrial smog, which emanated from the factory chimneys and furnaces of the adjacent iron-and-steel complex. Soon the sun's rays were totally extinguished, forcing me to reduce my speed and even switch on the car's headlights.

It was in these conditions that I pulled into the car park of the Pig Iron Arms, a large public house located immediately opposite the entrance gates of the factory complex. On entering I was greeted warmly by the publican and his rather large retinue of staff and was given a liquid nod from 'Jimmy', the sole customer. He introduced himself as he sat perched, swaying somewhat precariously, on a bar-room stool, looking decidedly the worse for wear with drink. However, what attracted my attention the most was the unusually long bar counter, which stretched the entire length of one side of the room. It must have measured over one hundred feet long by five feet wide, and would not have looked out of place in a Hollywood Western featuring the 'Golden Nugget' saloon − only the dancing girls and spittoons were missing! However, what was most extraordinary was that the entire surface of the bar counter was covered with dozens and dozens of recently filled, foaming pints of ale and yet, apart from myself and Jimmy, there were no other customers in the pub.

Just then the large clock on the wall behind the bar began to strike twelve noon and I detected a frisson of anticipation and a discernible quickening of movement and activity from the bar staff, who were scurrying behind the pint-strewn bar. On the last sonorous chime I became aware of a faint sound drifting through the open bar-room windows and then silence. I dismissed it from my mind and was about to approach the bar to order a snack lunch and query the massive display of ready-to-drink ale when there it was again! However, this time the distant sound seemed to be creeping closer and closer. I was reminded of that wonderful scene in the classic film *Zulu*, where the trapped Welsh Fusiliers at Rourke's Drift await the impending arrival of the Zulu massed army of warriors. A few more seconds elapsed and I was now somewhat alarmed at the ever-increasing cacophony of sound, which rumbled menacingly nearer and nearer; so much so that I retreated to a far corner seat of the bar to await the imminent arrival of the 'Zulu' army.

Suddenly, as the din reached a crescendo, the double doors crashed open and in poured a legion of jostling, vociferous, wild-eyed steel men, dressed in an assortment of sweaty, red-dusted overalls complete with soiled caps or various-coloured safety helmets and all wearing hob-nail boots, which collectively reproduced the staccato of the Zulus' 'spear on shield' battle cry. Realisation hit me: it was Friday, which meant it was payday. Within seconds the entire bar room was overflowing with sweating iron-and-steel workers who, armed with their week's wages, were desperate to replenish their dehydrated bodies as quickly as possible during their lunch break.

About an hour later, as the steel men slowly made their reluctant trek back to the furnaces to begin their afternoon shift, I returned to my automobile in the rear car park. Just as I was starting the ignition my attention was drawn to the forlorn figure of Jimmy, the 'worse for wear' drinker whom I had first encountered on my entry into the then nearly empty public house. He was staggering to the centre of the car park where the gents' public urinal was located. This structure was a large horseshoe-shaped sandstone outbuilding, with a tiled sign above the left entrance signifying 'In' and a corresponding tiled sign of 'Out' above the right entrance. In a cameo Chaplinesque scene straight out of a silent movie, Jimmy, whilst attempting to remain upright, was endeavouring to join the flow of the now-sated steel men who were urgent to relieve themselves and then return to their afternoon shift. Following several unsuccessful attempts to adhere himself to the moving tide of workers, Jimmy was suddenly lucky and was at last propelled through the 'In' entrance, only to emerge a few seconds later at the exit with a pained expression, still fiddling with his trousers' unopened fly buttons.

Shaking my head, I drove slowly out of the car park. I saw that Jimmy had unsuccessfully attempted the circuitous journey numerous times and, eventually succumbing to sheer exhaustion, had forgotten about his kidneys to lie down by the urinal wall to sleep!

Deep Freeze!

CHAPTER FIFTEEN

The Humming Bird

The Ideal Service Retail Company consisted of a couple of dozen small- to medium-sized grocery stores, located in and around Gateshead – a large northern town separated from the city of Newcastle by the River Tyne. Whether it was architecture, transport, shopping facilities or sporting activities, Gateshead was always regarded as the poorer cousin to the great city of Newcastle. As such, the town's civic leaders and inhabitants suffered from a corporate inferiority complex whenever they compared the merits of their own town to those of their superior neighbour across the Swing Bridge which straddled the dark coaly waters of the Tyne.

Nearly all the retail merchandise sold throughout the Ideal Service group, apart from perishable goods such as fruit and vegetables, was purchased centrally via the Ideal Service Company's administrative headquarters, located near the centre of town in Coatsworth Road. Responsibility for all aspects of the organisation was handled by the Buying Director, the Personnel Director and the Financial Director – and all these roles were carried out by one individual, Mr Bird (who rather coincidentally also happened to be the owner of the business, with a reputation in the local retail trade of being a somewhat eccentric entrepreneur and totally autocratic in the running of his fiefdom).

Following several boundary changes and the restructuring of different territories within my sales district, I found that my own area of responsibility had also widened. On top of my main workload, I was now put in charge of specific underperforming retail grocery companies as well – those that had apparent major business sales level problems. In other words, I was expected to be a troubleshooter and attempt to improve sales of the Thomas Hedley product range in certain retail accounts, those not generating their true volume potential. Number One on my troubleshooter hit list was the Ideal Service Retail Company Ltd. in Gateshead.

This company had been a puzzling underperformer for a while. The account background (the records maintained for all T. Hedley retail customers, which illustrated their monthly product purchasing patterns), together with my recent personal observations when visiting a few of the IS branches to get a feel for the company's in-store operation, indicated glaring out-of-stock situations. This was disastrous for my company as it meant we were losing important customer sales opportunities. Regarding this as an absolute priority, I accordingly telephoned the organisation and arranged a meeting with the owner as soon as possible.

So it was that the following Monday morning saw me parking outside the ISRC Headquarters on a raw, blustery December day, determined to resolve this particular retail account. With one last check of my sales aids equipment, together with a quick rehearsal of my intended presentation to the formidable Mr Bird, I leapt out of the car into a flurry of snowflakes and dashed for the warm, sheltered sanctuary of the office building. The sales aids I planned to use were designed to overcome any buyer resistance I might encounter, whilst simultaneously introducing the current enticing range of promotional offers (like reduced price packs – 3d off large Tide and Oxydol – plus a consumer offer of a free sponge banded to every special carton of Flash). The *pièce de résistance* of my sales aids was a seasonal trade-buying incentive cash bonus for any quantity of Mirro Scouring Powder ordered and delivered that December. I was sure that these offers would be tempting enough to resolve the low volume business we had with Ideal Service.

Apart from these incentives, I was also in possession of various dummy product cartons as visual samples of the promoted brands (these always had a greater impact on any buy/sell situation and were a huge improvement on simply presenting details of the proposition on sheets of paper, however elegantly typed from the Sales Office).

In my previous evening's preparation I had been shocked to discover the full extent of the situation: not only were several of Thomas Hedley's leading brands not stocked at Ideal Service stores, but IS was purchasing nowhere near its true volume potential for such a large group of retail outlets.

Why? I hoped to find out the answer to this mystery in my forthcoming meeting with Mr Bird.

I was somewhat apprehensive on entering the building's foyer, as this was to be my first encounter with the redoubtable owner of Ideal Service. However, as always, my adrenalin was flowing and I was looking forward to the anticipated confrontational challenge ahead of me. I bustled my way through the swing doors and presented myself at the reception desk. If possible, the reception area was colder than the wintry inhospitable weather I had left outside: it was as if I had entered an igloo!

The receptionist (Nancy – whom I later christened Nanook) was a somewhat elderly lady, smothered in a heavy threadbare fur coat and a bright red woollen scarf. Her ensemble was completed with matching fur fingerless gloves, which revealed red bony extremities. Her wrinkled face peeped out from under her Arctic protective attire as I entered the reception area. After introducing myself, Nancy asked me to take a seat on a row of classroom-type benches. She then proceeded to jump up and down and curse venomously, all her anger directed towards her employer, Mr Bird, who from what I quickly gathered was a 'penny-pinching, miserly skinflint' who made Scrooge appear to be a kind and generous benefactor. Apparently he underpaid all his staff, refused permission to switch on the office and adjoining warehouse's central heating system and grudgingly only allowed paraffin heaters to be placed near the building's plumbing areas to avoid the danger of frozen and burst pipes.

On and on the wretched woman continued, only for her vituperation to be interrupted suddenly by the shrill ring from an internal telephone on her desk. Within seconds I was being ushered through a large glass door and, following the receptionist at a sprint (so this was how she kept warm!), down several freezing corridors. I was finally catapulted through an imposing frosted (naturally) glass door, stencilled 'Private', and into the sanctum of Mr Bird, about whom I was becoming more and more curious.

The sub-zero temperature in the office matched the igloo conditions prevailing in the reception area. The room was sparsely furnished and dimly lit. Large, gloomy-looking wood panels dominated the interior, along with a huge, impressive, richly polished mahogany desk. The sash windows had not been acquainted with a chamois leather for years and, despite the temperature, one of the windows was ajar, allowing the odd errant snowflake to drift into the room. Somehow, I had envisaged the autocratic Mr B. to be a large, physically dominant individual, but to my utter astonishment he was neither. Instead, seated behind the massive desk and perched on a raised swivel leather chair sat a tiny man, enveloped in a haze of cigarette smoke, with only his head and shoulders visible. Mr Bird possessed a healthy somewhat ruddy complexion, with dark, sleeked-back brilliantined hair. He was the height of sartorial elegance with a well-cut pinstriped suit, blue shirt and polka-dotted bow tie. The cigarette in his mouth remained firmly attached as if it were welded to his lower lip. Even as he talked, the glowing Woodbine seemed to defy gravity, occasionally cascading white ash across the highly polished surface of the desk and onto his well-tailored suit lapels.

Before I could introduce myself, Mr Bird exclaimed in a broad squeaky Geordie accent, 'Morning, Thomas Hedley – my time is precious and time is money, so get on with it.' Sensing a fast introduction was required, I dispensed with the usual 'get to know you, rotten weather' opening chat and launched straightaway into my presentation of the promotional offers, emphasising the additional business that would be generated, so benefiting his company. However following only a few seconds of my introduction, Mr B. suddenly pivoted in his swivel chair towards the open window, took several deep intakes of the chilled air and to my consternation commenced to sing! Well, to be accurate, it was more of a hum and, with a somewhat dismissive wave of his hand, he beckoned me to continue as the strains of the once popular Victorian tune 'Red Sails in the Sunset' filled the room and he focused his attention on the panoramic view from the open window.

For the first time since my early training period, I was flummoxed. Attempting to discuss a detailed business proposition (with the use of various visual effective sales aids) to a buyer's back whilst competing with a melancholic tune proved somewhat daunting. Nevertheless, taking a deep breath, I carried on, ignoring the melody. After a one-way conversation, which seemed to last an eternity, I completed my presentation. A few seconds elapsed before the humming also abated and silence ensued. Then my adversary swivelled to face me at last and exclaimed in his reedy voice, 'Reet! That's it then. Leave your proposition with my receptionist on your way oot! We'll be in touch.' Mr Bird then promptly pressed a button on the corner of the desk, offered me a handshake and, before I could utter a word, the office door flew open and I found myself catapulted out of the room by 'Nanook'. Within seconds I was being unceremoniously bundled into the reception area, relieved of the relevant documents and shown into the car park. I glanced at my watch: from entering the building to exiting, it had been all of twelve minutes!

One week later, my sales office confirmed that they had received an order from Ideal Service, but on analysing their purchases it became apparent that the levels of merchandise ordered had fallen way below expectation. Indeed, for such a large group of retail outlets the volume requested was derisory, which in turn meant a continuation of this organisation's poor performance with regard to our brands.

The New Year was soon upon us. January, February, March, April and May went by, and my monthly calls to the Ideal Service Retail Company all continued to follow a standard pattern: the humming and being ignored followed by a terribly low order. No matter how I tried to vary the interview, Mr 'Red Sails in the Sunset' refused to tack in my direction! June came and, six months since the day of my first encounter with Mr Bird, I found myself yet again in the reception area of the ISRC. Nearly two seasons had flown by, and Nancy (Nanook no longer appropriate), instantly recognising me, welcomed me for my appointment. She was no longer the trussed-up Eskimo of some months previous and indeed wore an attractive floral dress, on which I complimented her. This in no way deterred her from launching into the now traditional scathing indictment of her employer.

A few minutes later in the owner's sanctum I was sure enough greeted by, 'Morning, Thomas Hedley – my time is precious and time is money, so get on with it.' Then, true to form, Mr Bird swivelled his chair, gazed out of the open window, and 'Red Sails in the Sunset' soon drifted out on the air.

I was desperate, and had had enough. Trying something new, I sat absolutely still and was as quiet as a church mouse. After a short while an odd silence crept throughout the room as Mr Bird's rendering slowly died away. Yet this was soon followed by the humming of a differently pitched tune, 'Blow the Wind Southerly'. This time, however, the melody came not from Mr B.'s lips, but mine! I had decided to join in the impromptu concert and continued to hum as I gazed out of the window. Several minutes elapsed before my fellow chorister slowly swivelled around, faced me with a whimsical expression and, with a broad smile, exclaimed, ' "Blow the Wind Southerly"? That's one of my favourite songs!' He then proceeded to sing the first few verses with gusto. After this rendition he told me that he was a stalwart of the local Gateshead Music Society and, indeed, their president. Fortunately, with my church choirboy musical background I was at last able to establish a rapport with Mr B., albeit through a melodious conduit.

There then followed a deep discussion on the merits of my favourite hymn ('Jesu, Joy of Man's Desiring') until we eventually refocused on the 'Soapy Business' at hand. After some tough negotiations, I agreed to a change in my company's product distribution operation, whereby all future deliveries would be sent to individual IS branches rather than to their warehouse: this in effect saved Mr Bird's organisation storage and distribution overheads, whilst at the same time allowing Thomas Hedley salesmen into each store, where they would be able to negotiate all future supplies with the individual shop managers.

I was euphoric. Triumph! I had finally made a breakthrough after six barren months of monosyllabic contact. I waltzed into the reception area and gave the indomitable Nancy a celebratory peck on the cheek on my way out. Blushing, she scolded me and, threatening to tell her husband, bade me farewell. And, I discovered some months later that her full name was Nancy Bird – the wife of the boss!

Hasty Retreat

CHAPTER SIXTEEN

Change of Pace

As in most occupations, the months can appear to literally fly by when you are enjoying every minute of the working day. After nearly three years carrying the capacious leather bag full of Thomas Hedley soap samples across the threshold of the retail grocers throughout the North East of England, I was now a confident and successful section salesman, winner of several District Sales Competitions. I was really enjoying working in the grocery trade despite the occasional resistance and flak thrown at me by the man in the brown coat. I had found my niche in life.

Also, the Company policy of trading-in salesmen's automobiles and replacing them with brand new models every three-year period meant that I was now the proud driver of the ubiquitous Morris 1000 (Reg. BVK 182), whose distinctive throaty 'baffled' exhaust emission, together with its short sporty gear stick, transformed the driver into a potential Monte Carlo contestant. I can still clearly recall racing home from Carlisle one late Friday afternoon in competition with John Scott, and arriving in the city of Newcastle in less than an hour (a distance of over sixty miles) without the benefit of dual carriageways. By now I was engaged to the beautiful Judy and, with my future secure as a permanent salesman with the Procter & Gamble organisation (the

Thomas Hedley Company name now obsolete), there appeared to be not a cloud on the horizon.

Then, suddenly, one day out of the blue I received a memo from my boss J.W. Caygill, instructing me to report to his office on the following Friday morning. I was immediately convinced that trouble lay ahead, for an invitation to J.W.'s sanctum was generally interpreted as a visit that meant you were to be either hired or fired! So, seated outside the great man's office, I attempted to eliminate the reasons which perhaps could justify why my career was to be terminated. Certainly my sales performance over the past couple of years was excellent. I had won several District Sales and Display Competitions and, since the unfortunate company automobile write-off, my driving record had been unblemished (despite my Monte Carlo inclinations). Furthermore, to my knowledge there had been no individual complaints from any of my retail customers – not even a peep from Mr and Mrs Tallentires' Cumberland Co-op! And, surely, too much water had flowed under the bridge for someone in the Personnel Department to have unearthed and analysed the accuracy of my original job application form from some three years ago.

Still speculating, I entered the illustrious man's office and all was quickly revealed when I received a reassuring pat on the back from a smiling J.W. He introduced me to the third person in the room: Norman Riley, the Company's Sales Training Manager, who was based at Procter & Gamble's administrative headquarters, located a few miles outside of Newcastle in the town of

Gosforth. I was then given the totally surprising news that I had been chosen to attend a fortnight's training course the following month at the Company's Head Office. This in effect meant that I had been selected to become a Company Trainer, soon to be responsible for the initial training of new recruits within the Sales Department, and this was the first step on Procter & Gamble's pyramidal management ladder. I was astonished – promotion!

To date I had achieved, in just under three years, all of the personal objectives I had set myself some years ago when, as a lowly office boy, I had dreamed of fame and fortune. Amongst these ambitions had been the owning of a motorcar (with the status that accompanied it), escorting a beautiful film star (read: the delectable Judy, my then fiancée and now wonderful wife), an agreeable and healthy salary and, most important of all, having been brought up in a working-class post-war austere environment, job security. All of these I had achieved – and within such a short space of time. I therefore looked no further than to continue holding down my salesman's job to the best of my ability right up until my retirement, when I could enjoy the projected, excellent Procter & Gamble pension.

In a daze, I bade my farewell and walked out of the Sales Office into the street outside, the congratulations of my boss and the staff ringing in my ears. I found it difficult to absorb the enormity of such an unexpected opportunity which had just been presented to me. I realised I would now have to take my job really seriously! No longer was I one of the lads, and I wondered whether this would herald the end of my swashbuckling selling approach and my theatrical in-store performances, now that I was being groomed for management. The majority of my fellow salesmen were senior employees in terms of service – how would they react to the elevation of my role as Sales Trainer?

However, I soon discovered that though I had been astounded by my promotion, the general consensus of opinion from my senior colleagues was a grudging, 'We thought that you were next in line', and that was that. What I didn't realise, however, was that from the moment J.W. Caygill had slapped me on the back and offered me his congratulations, my life was to change dramatically.

The two-week Sales Trainers' Course passed swiftly and I arrived back at my sales district office totally motivated and looking forward to my first training assignment, which would give me the responsibility of introducing a freshly recruited trainee to the world of the 'Soapy Business'. The Trainers' Course covered all aspects of the salesman's field operation comprehensively, together with teaching the techniques and skills required to gradually introduce a trainee into his new competitive environment.

The whole emphasis of the training programme had been designed to enable the trainee to hit the ground running. The new employee would accompany his trainer into a store from day one, so that he could observe at first hand the format of the in-store selling procedure. Each store visit was then immediately followed by an analysis with the trainer on the merits and results of the sales call. This was generally held in the confines of his 'office' (the company car) or perhaps over several cups of coffee in a nearby café. Then, over the next few days the trainee took on more and more responsibility for his own store visits (still under supervision) until he was deemed capable of handling his sales calls solo.

Being taught the duties of a trainer brought back my memories of the time three years before (so long?) when I had been the untutored newcomer. Now I got to see the experience from the other side and was soon conversant in how to carry out, among other things, the countless charade training sessions. (Oh, those charades! Re-experiencing them made me realise how much I had progressed in such a short time.)

It was not long before I was assigned my first training responsibility, in Sunderland. This was several miles south of my district sales office in Newcastle. The trainee's name was Norman Pigg – a delightful, tall and intelligent former schoolteacher, who excelled as a cricketer in the local area and had a reputation as a formidable fast bowler. It transpired that he was frustrated by the lack of promotional opportunities and, indeed, the poor financial rewards available within the teaching profession at that time. He was recently married and hungry for success in a new career, plus there was the undoubted attraction of working for an organisation that supplied a motorcar, a luxury unaffordable on his meagre teaching salary.

The first few days of training seemed to pass quite smoothly and Norman absorbed all aspects of the introductory programme with real panache. He possessed a ready wit and we became firm friends (especially as he responded so quickly to my training approach – and to my sense of humour). Eventually, the first important milestone arrived: Norman's first in-store sales call, where I would take on an observer's role only. During the past few days, Norman had grown immeasurably in confidence and was straining at the leash to be given the opportunity to assume control of his own store visits. Our recent calls to various emporiums had become sure and practised and these were now always followed by excellent charade sessions.

So, we arrived outside a small grocery outlet located in the Pennywell area of the town – a well-populated suburb of council-owned properties – for Norman's big test. Prior to entering the store, we double-checked the previous evening's planned sales and merchandising targets for this particular store. Then, with a deep intake of breath, Norman leapt out of the car and strode briskly towards the shop, carrying his leather sample bag and several items of cardboard in-store display material. I followed discreetly in his footsteps, confident that Norman would do well. We entered the emporium, where the proprietor was just finishing serving a customer. In his determination to make a good impression, my trainee promptly tripped over a sack of potatoes, fell heavily against the departing customer and unceremoniously knocked the unfortunate housewife to the floor! I groaned. Was this a portent of things to follow?

Annoyed that her somewhat flushed and departing customer had had to limp painfully from the store, the owner, Mrs Hogg – coincidentally a rather large, porcine, buxom woman with flared nostrils – glared at my unfortunate trainee and snorted, 'Ye clumsy bugga! Whee the hell are yee and what dee you want?'

Immediately I sensed that Norman had lost the plot. His eyes seemed to glaze over as he picked himself up, together with his display material which was strewn across the sawdusted floor, and he looked imploringly at me for assistance. As in all dramas on the stage, when the leading man forgets his lines, he momentarily dies. And at that moment, centre stage left, Norman had painfully died and was speechlessly awaiting the assistance of the prompter!

My sales experience over the past few years had taught me that when handling the unpredictable, often confrontational, behaviour of the grocer, one of the best things to do is to introduce drama or humour to the situation. I had usually been able to extract myself from tricky situations doing this – a diversionary technique I had tried to impart throughout the training sessions with my trainee, but in his panic none of this advice seemed to have rubbed off on Norman. I hoped he would soon remember it, so, ignoring my trainee's plight, I walked to the rear of the store and pretended to examine a basket of overripe bananas. At last Norman seemed to compose himself and, dusting himself down, turned to face his adversary. Instead of following the standard sales introduction, as rehearsed throughout our many previous charade training sessions, he deviated from the script completely. To my alarm he jokingly introduced himself to the formidable Mrs H. in a timorous voice, as follows: 'Ah! Good morning Mrs Hogg, we might be related. My name's Pigg. Do you mind if we trot into your cellar and check your stock?'

There was a deathly silence in the store, interrupted only by the large clock on the wall behind the counter striking ten o'clock – as if a timekeeper at a boxing booth was counting out the losing contestant. I held my breath. Mrs H. did not seem to realise that there really was a genuine Mr Pigg standing in front of her. We later speculated that maybe she felt she was being mocked by this unfortunate farmyard poetical comparison, or perhaps it was her 'time of the month', or even maybe that her husband had recently run off with the young barmaid at the Pennywell Arms. Whatever the reason, Mrs H. erupted! With a torrent of colourful invective, she screamed, 'Get oot! Get oot! Caal me a pig, I'll ave yer guts for garters!' and then proceeded to bombard us with the nearest items of merchandise from the serving counter: bread buns, tins of sardines, boxes of clothes pegs and finally, just as we scrambled to the shop door, a large turnip, which Norman (the cricketer) caught brilliantly right-handed.

Sprinting down the street as fast as the bulky equipment we were carrying would allow, and to the consternation of several passers-by, we eventually reached the sanctuary of the company car and piled in like two getaway bank robbers, the car engine revving furiously as we made our escape. Eventually we parked outside the local café and, recovering from our recent explosive ordeal over several cups of coffee, admired the 'prize turnip' Norman had caught, which we later gave to the café owner. Laughing, with tears in our eyes, we analysed the previous embarrassing events and accepted that sprawling in the store on entering was not exactly conducive to a smooth store introduction. Certainly, the choice of the agricultural metaphor was unfortunate to say the least.

Still, I am pleased to record that the remainder of the day passed quite uneventfully and my trainee was able to put the 'Mrs Hogg' incident behind him. To his credit he completed the rest of that day's workload efficiently, including successfully carrying out his first 'solo' store sales call without the benefit of the trainer's presence. However, that evening during the charade sessions, I emphasised that while the selective application of humour was still a useful conduit in overcoming a confrontational situation with the grocer, perhaps in the future the use of certain farmyard similes should be avoided. A point Norman heeded for the rest of his career!

The Rock

CHAPTER SEVENTEEN

Viva La Gibraltar

The promotional pyramid at Procter & Gamble involved eight layers of management – from the lowly sales trainee to the post of Company Sales Director. Over the years I was astonished every time I received a promotion: so much so that I often wondered what criteria the Company must have used when they elevated me to the next rung of the ladder. Certainly my sales performance during my career was more than useful, yet so were the sales results of many of my colleagues. My track record for producing outstanding sales trainees was excellent, and yet there were also other high-calibre trainers. I did gel reasonably well with my fellow co-workers, possessed a good sense of humour and was diligent in all aspects of my work: still, there must have been many sales personnel who matched me. In retrospect, the only area of my sales management where perhaps I may have been ahead of the pack was my ability to create and implement new promotional ideas. These ranged over the years from Billy Webster's 'Soap Clinic', in my early days of employment, to successful major feature events I sold to important high street retail organisations involving hundreds of stores.

It was ten years since I had made my first sale to the Cheesey emporium. I had moved miraculously through

165

the Company's management structure and was now a National District Sales Manager in the National Accounts Division. This meant that I had reached the sixth level of the Company's promotional pyramid. At this rarefied height, I had the responsibility for P&G's overall business of several major UK retail organisations, including Boots, F.W. Woolworths and Asda, plus several other smaller retail corporations. My new job involved calling at the headquarters of these clients, often several times each month, and establishing a good personal relationship with each of the retail-buying executives. This frequently meant socialising outside office hours (wining and dining at various trade functions) and I was able to develop a sound personal relationship with each of the various decision makers.

It took only a few weeks for me to recognise that the necessary criteria required to succeed in this senior management position were not too different from the basic selling techniques I had honed many years ago, selling to the small corner-shop grocer. The principles were exactly the same: the only differences were the volume size of orders negotiated (e.g., ten thousand cases as opposed to ten cases) and the fact that often the bureaucratic purchasing executive did not possess a fraction of the commonsense held by the independent small-town retailer. So, to succeed at this level of business I realised I would need to introduce more than the normal level of drama I had used as a lowly salesman. It became apparent that to win large orders from these accounts would require something extra.

It didn't take long for me to also understand that if a manufacturer of a major consumer brand were to offer an exclusive promotion to only one retail organisation, then that product would get guaranteed maximum in-store priority from that particular retailer. Moreover, the extra stock delivered to support the 'exclusive' promotion would receive massive in-store exposure and indeed national press advertising (often funded by the retailer). Now, all I needed to do was to be able to use this new insight to acquire some large orders.

However, at that time Procter & Gamble, with its incredibly strong stable of mass-advertised household brands, operated a rigid UK trading policy. All of its UK promotional activity had to be identical, without any variation, and its monthly cycle of consumer offers to the trade – like a free sponge with Flash or 3d off Tide – were made available to all of its retail and wholesale customers (during the same planned period of time) on a 'take it or leave it' basis. In other words there were no exclusive, tailor-made promotions available to any one single organisation. So, with a view to generating extra business, I decided to introduce a degree of 'layered' exclusivity to my accounts – without compromising my company's promotional policy. To do this I would need to persuade one of my major clients to use their own budget to introduce greater consumer impact on P&G merchandise. The retail organisation I decided to make the target of my efforts was the one which boasted the largest number of outlets on the UK high street with over one thousand stores: F.W. Woolworths.

So, determined to make my idea work, I knew I would have to suggest something really spectacular if I were to get this giant retailer enthusiastic about a special promotional effort. After some thought, it came to me: the launch of a high-profile competition exclusive to Woolworths – tied in to P&G products of course – would be an ideal proposal; one that would be sure to get their backing. All I needed to do was to come up with a competition desirable enough to the consumer to make it a huge success.

My strategy took me to Gibraltar. At that time the question of the sovereignty of Gibraltar was big news and I quickly saw that if I could only link this issue into the promotion then it could cash in on the current massive hype that was occurring. (Indeed, the veiled threats of Spain for the return of Gibraltar – whose inhabitants regarded themselves as British – were not only having a huge impact in Britain, but were also making headlines worldwide.) With this in mind I made Gibraltar the focus of the competition: the top prizes would be twenty free holidays to Gibraltar, its desirability as a destination backed up by the enormous pro-British feeling the sovereignty issue was creating. Eye-catching in-store displays showing 'the Rock' as the perfect British holiday venue could be displayed throughout the UK, the 'We are British' Union Jack message emblazoned across the one-thousand-plus Woolworths high street stores. Millions of leaflets printed to highlight the desirable prizes to Woolworths' shoppers would further publicise the competition. To top this all off, the P&G/Woolworths

promotion could be highlighted in a national press advertising campaign.

The only obstacle was funding. The prizes were ambitiously expensive. How would I get Woolworths to agree to pay for it all?

On my own initiative I contacted the Gibraltan Tourist Department and, following my proposal, was referred to the Minister of Tourism, Pepe Vaughan. After several communications I found myself flying out to Gibraltar – much to the chagrin of some of my colleagues. At a meeting with certain members of the cabinet, I waxed lyrical about my proposed promotion, where the Britishness of Gibraltar could be used as the focus of a massive retail campaign. The timing for Gibraltar couldn't be better: for a sizeable contribution to the promotional budget (a sum which they could easily afford), Gibraltar would be the recipient of enormous pro-British publicity. My plan was given unanimous approval and I was delighted. With this substantial backing I was confident enough to go to Woolworths with my scheme. Their agreement to participate in my 'layered' promotion was not long in coming. Triumph! I had my funding!

So, the entire expenses for the campaign – the extra display material, the press advertising, the consumer holidays and the British Airways flights from the UK – were handled by the budgets of the Gibraltar Government and the Woolworths organisation. Procter & Gamble's only contribution was to guarantee that every participating store had sufficient stock of merchandise to meet the anticipated extra demand and that the field sales force would be on hand to assist with the in-store display activities.

When the campaign launched, I waited anxiously to see what would happen. Was my initiative going to pay off? To my joy, the campaign was a huge success and July 1974 became a record business month for P&G in Woolworths.

Riding high on such an achievement, I decided to repeat this strategy a few months later. I proposed a new campaign, again with the Woolworths organisation (who had been delighted with the results of the first promotion). However, this time the competition partner was the Honda Motor Company, who donated two brand-new Accord motorcars and thirty motorised scooters as the major prizes for the consumer competition (which was linked, of course, to the condition of proof of purchase of various P&G products). Honda were a keen participant because at that time they were just feeling their way into the UK saloon car market (they had a very limited dealer distribution network) and in return for supporting the campaign they would receive massive exposure for their cars and motorcycles across every town in the UK where a Woolworths store was located. As an extra bonus to this promotion, Honda would also be able to place an actual showroom Honda car or scooter in virtually every store as the centrepiece of a P&G product display. The Honda Motor Company were thrilled – as was I. October 1974 proved to be another record month for P&G in Woolworths!

Following such stunning success, I was invited to participate that year in Procter & Gamble's annual Sales Management Conference. P&G were keen to highlight the potential extra business that could be generated from the creation of further similar feature events across a wider range of our key retail customers. To dramatise this point – and inspire my sales colleagues – it was agreed that I would participate in an on-stage charade highlighting my promotional ideas and, to add real impact to the proceedings, I would begin my presentation by arriving on the platform astride a Honda motorised scooter – complete with racing leathers and a Geoff Duke crash helmet! This theatrical stunt was to be the showstopper of the conference and a fitting climax for the end of the symposium.

However, I had never ridden a motorcycle before. Keen to give it a go, I jumped on the scooter in the venue's car park and proceeded to wobble my way around the parking lot. After a few circuits – and bumps – of the car park, I had soon grasped the simple technique of start, clutch, brake and accelerator. My dramatic entry into the conference theatre was to involve me roaring down the centre aisle from the foyer, up a steep ramp and onto the centre of the stage. Then, after parking the bike, and with a final rev of the two-stroke cylinder engine, I was to leap off the saddle, divest myself of my 'Grand Prix' racing leathers and launch into my presentation, with the well-rehearsed words, 'Gentlemen! Why not join me in the Formula One fast lane and outstrip our competitors with similar amazing eye-catching promotions!'

Alas, on my cue, signalling my agreed entrance into the auditorium, the Honda 'Express' scooter stubbornly refused to start! Stuck in the foyer, I was anxious to arrive on time and synchronise my entrance with the announcer's enthusiastic welcome. With few moments to spare, I decided to push the reluctant motorcycle into the arena and freewheel down the centre aisle instead. However, picking up speed, I careened into the ramp leading up to the raised stage and promptly cartwheeled into the orchestra pit. Disaster! Desperate to recover from my unplanned stage entry, I collected my thoughts quickly and, ignoring the throbbing bruises, stoically carried out my presentation – which was greeted with a mixture of laughter and applause. After the conference, I vowed never to get on a motorcycle again! They do say that, in the world of the theatre, actors should avoid working with children or animals – well, I would like to add temperamental motorcycles to that list!

Hasty Exit!

EPILOGUE

Déjà Vu

My career with Proctor & Gamble spanned over two decades, and during that time I managed to move successfully up the UK sales management structure. Not only was this rewarding in financial terms, it was also laced with a certain amount of job satisfaction. Such was my dedication that even on family holidays – be it in Cornwall or Malta – I would check out the status of P&G's products being stocked at the local stores (much to the resigned amusement of my family)!

However, for all my achievements, my fondest memories are for the early stages of my career. Those initial days of often confrontational jousting for relatively tiny orders stood me in good stead for the competitive, and frequently theatrical, atmosphere of negotiating with UK retail supermarket giants for orders valued at hundreds of thousands of pounds. And of all the places I have worked in over the years, I still retain a deep affection for the district which comprised my first sales sector...

Nearly twenty years had passed since those early Thomas Hedley selling adventures and I found myself back in my original sales region once again. Together with my family – Judy and our three sons (not triplets!) – I was travelling en route to the Lake District for an autumn holiday. I was looking forward to revisiting such a beautiful area, which would by now be at its most seductive and glorious. We had stopped in the town of Barnard Castle – partially as a result of my family's demands to stretch their legs after a long car journey, but mainly in response to the clamouring appeals for Coca-Cola and barley sugar sweets – and I found myself standing outside the local grocer's store of Cheeseborough and Son (the proprietor's name now in rather faded gold lettering above the shop window). I was pleasantly surprised to discover the store was still under the same ownership and curious to see what changes I would find in the shop after so many years.

A bell tinkled when I entered the store and the owner of the emporium looked up from his dealings with the only other occupant: a salesman. I could instantly recognise him as such by his laptop computer and the various product samples and documents which were strewn across the serving counter. The poor rep was immediately dismissed to one side with a disdainful wave of the proprietor's hand, before the owner turned to me, replacing a scowl with a benign smile. Mr Cheeseborough (son of Edam, I assumed) then ushered me forward towards the serving area in an unctuous manner. Déjà vu! It seemed suddenly as if only weeks had passed since my last visit to this retail store and yet here I was in the role of a 'valuable' customer.

To my great satisfaction I managed to astonish the proprietor by telling him I was in no desperate hurry for my requirements and that he should finish his negotiations with the rep, adding (somewhat tongue-in-cheek) that without the services of the manufacturer's representative, perhaps he would not be in business today. Cheesey Junior gave me a puzzled look and reluctantly recommenced his negotiations with the salesman. Looking around the store I could see that not much had changed. Apart from the bacon-slicing machine (which I noticed was no longer manually operated), and an attempt to introduce more of a self-service element into the shop (via a free-standing unit allowing customers to choose their own biscuits from open-topped tins), the layout of the interior of the store seemed just the same as it had in my early selling days.

Suddenly the plastic curtains leading into the rear of the premises parted and in hobbled Himself: the older but still recognisable figure of Mr Cheeseborough Senior. Giving his protégé a withering glance, he addressed me with a quizzical look and a rubbing of hands before saying, 'Now, sir, what can my esteemed establishment offer you today?' Then, after a slight pause and with a suspicious gleam in his eye, he added, 'Haven't we met somewhere before?' Remembering my deception of so many years ago when, on my first solo visit, I had invented the existence of a wife with newborn triplets, I was highly embarrassed. I declined to acknowledge our previous encounters and promptly gave my order for drinks and confectionery, sure my face was turning red. After paying Cheesey Senior, I thanked him quickly and exited the store. My sigh of relief was premature, however, as just as I was closing the door a voice rang out behind me with 'Give my regards to the wife and triplets!'

As I made my escape, I couldn't help but wonder whether my ruse had been seen through after all. Had the proprietor's tone been a touch ironic? I shook my head as I headed back to the car. On reflection, I realised that, even though I might have prevailed in many a negotiation with the man in the brown coat behind the counter, it still never pays to underestimate that most formidable of opponents – the indomitable grocer!

'And so – ending now, having told my tale . . .

*I have been a Town Traveller and a Country Traveller.
I was always on the road and, literally speaking, I was
always wandering here and there . . . about the city streets
and the country by-roads – seeing many little things and some
great things . . .*

*. . . Things that happened during wonderful, never-to-be-
repeated, carefree days and, because they have interested me, I
hope they have interested others.*

*These, then, are my brief credentials as the
Uncommercial Traveller.'*

John Solomon
1934–